Infinite Ways to Stay Creative

Jessie Gao

First published by Busybird Publishing 2025

Copyright © 2025 Jessie Gao

ISBN
Print: 978-1-923216-77-8
Ebook: 978-1-923216-78-5

This work is copyright. Apart from any use permitted under the Copyright Act 1968, no part of this publication may be reproduced, stored in a retrieval system or transmitted in any form or by any means, electronic, mechanical, photocopying, recording or otherwise, without the prior written permission of Jessie Gao.

The information in this book is based on the author's experiences and opinions. The author and publisher disclaim responsibility for any adverse consequences, which may result from use of the information contained herein. Permission to use any external content has been sought by the author. Any breaches will be rectified in further editions of the book.

Cover image: Busybird Publishing

Cover design: Busybird Publishing

Layout and typesetting: Busybird Publishing

Illustrations: Jessie Gao

Busybird Publishing
2/118 Para Road
Montmorency, Victoria
Australia 3094
www.busybird.com.au

APPENDIX

Hello there! Our creative journey starts here. Yes I know it says Appendix, but this book is about challenging how you think.

The first rule is: You're not allowed to start reading from the end of this book – it will ruin the pleasure of reading it.

Are you ready...

If I say, '**DO NOT** picture a **PINK BOOK** for the next 5 minutes', I bet you've already pictured a pink book in your mind and for the next 5 minutes, you won't be able to get the book image out of your head. Is the **PINK BOOK** still stuck in your mind right now?

It's not your fault. I'm the same. I've been trying to tell myself not to think about a pink book, even any book while writing this sentence. My inner voice started to yell out to me, loud and clear, 'book', 'book', 'book', 'pink', 'pink', 'pink'. I seem unable to delete an image of the book and the colour from my head.

Have you formed a picture of your book, the one I told you not to think about? Like: What's the shape of the book (square, round, triangle, heart, rectangle, etc.)? What colour is the front and back cover? Is it still PINK? Does the book have a title? What's the genre of the book? Is it a completely new genre that doesn't exist yet? Is it a book that you've read or one that hasn't been written yet, or maybe just this book that you're holding in your hand, the one that you're curious about? Is it a book that you wrote, edited, designed and published, or is it written by Artificial Intelligence (AI), partially or completely? Is it just one book or a stack of books stuck in your mind?

I bet you are thinking, "Seriously, what do you want me to learn through this 'picturing a book' activity?" (Well, why did you crack open this book in the first place? You tell me.)

Is the book picture still in your mind?

APPENDIX

The second rule here: At the end of each chapter, make a summary of what you've learnt. But your challenge is, you can only use five words. Should we call it a chapter? Or shall we have a fun game renaming each 'chapter' of a book as something else? What could you possibly give the chapter of a book a new name? Write your answers below (as many as possible):

_____

_____

_____

I hope these questions have started to keep you engaged and somehow activated your creative brainpower. If you'd like super-big challenges, try NOT even starting any 'chapter' just yet – think of this *Infinite (∞) Ways to Stay Creative* as your own book, what would be your book structure? What would you put in the book to show your fellow creators the techniques, ways, approaches to remain creative throughout their lifetime.

The third rule about reading this book: *Infinite (∞) Ways to Stay Creative*? Well, create a fun rule for yourself in the blank area below.

_____

_____

_____

The interesting, weird rules that I imagine you possibly put down, or maybe not:

- ∞ have my pants (shirt) on whenever I touch the book
- ∞ share this book with my closest friend today
- ∞ read out every second word

- ∞ flick through odd pages only and take a guess on what the even pages could be talking about
- ∞ highlight words of 'creativity' and 'creative' throughout the book.

How about 'no third rules at all'? There are already too many rules for me to handle in daily life, and I don't have to take on any nonsense or meaningless rules.

I hope these three activities have started you on your creative journey.

Now let's take a break and complete the boardgame on the back cover. You can:

- ∞ add a verb in front of ∞
- ∞ change the dice into cuboid shape
- ∞ make the dice into a maximum of 8 dots on one of the sides
- ∞ delete or extend the squares
- ∞ remove useless words or steps
- ∞ do whatever you'd like.

Do whatever you'd like. Yeah, you're absolutely right! I probably will colour it, ditch the whole back cover and stick on a brand-new design, or just do nothing (Why do I have to follow your instructions), or what else?

Congratulations! You've just explored your creative nature! Do you even realise that there are so many ideas that you can come up, even just with a book's back cover or just the choice of the text font, size or how it gets presented.

After you've read the book, come back and design your own board game or design the best and most perfect back cover for the book in the blank area on the next page. Do not just picture it in your

APPENDIX

mind, as brilliant ideas disappear instantly if you don't write them down immediately (See Topic 25). This is the exercise that I'd like you do. All ideas are welcome, and all ideas are gems!

It's a tradition to choose either American English or British English spellings for a book, e.g. color vs. colour, recognize vs. recognise, traveler vs. traveller. Why can't we break the rule and bring a bit fun in the book? British English spelling is used across the book except the word 'colour/color'. I deliberately spell **colour/color** in the two ways in the book, go find them!

By now, is the **PINK BOOK** picture still in your mind?

END

Dear creators, welcome to the end section of the book! Wait! Did I 'hear' that wrong? We just opened the book, and we've already got to the end section?

No, you didn't 'hear' it wrong. Have you heard this quote: 'Every new beginning comes from some other beginning's end?' In this section, I'm going to share with you on my first book creating experience.

My creative writing journey starts from here (The beginning):

In June 2017 – I typed the first word for my first book on my laptop.

One year on – I had 80,000 words. I kept going.

Two years on – A 'book' with almost 180,000 words was completed! Keep going!

Three years on – I edited it myself, three times. I received a 12-page manuscript assessment, which suggested I change the structure for the whole book. Gees! Should I just keep going! Reality? I wanted to give up millions of times already – publishing a book is hard. It's a creativity (extremely fun part) plus administration (extremely detail driven and time-consuming). But I've come thus far, and there's no reason not to keep going.

Four years on – I almost completely restructured the book and reworked each page.

Five years later – After working with my editors for three-rounds of editing, rewriting pages and paragraphs again, again and again, plus numerous checks of each word, and the punctuation, the book finally came into shape.

In November 2022, my first book *The English Builder!: Ace your English in 365 Days* (about 150,000 words, 408 pages in the end) was finally released on Amazon and other online bookshops globally!

Infinite Ways to Stay Creative

Phew!!

Phew∞∞∞∞∞∞∞∞∞∞∞∞∞∞∞∞∞∞∞∞∞∞∞∞∞∞∞∞∞∞∞∞

Below emojis presented most of my whole writing experiences and self-publishing process, if not all of it.

😊😃🤓🤨🤔💤😕☹️🤭🙂😀😅😇😨😠😇😌😐

😂🤣😁😉😎😒😡😔😍🙃😪😦😰😳🥰😗🤗😆

(And repeat, for billions of times during the five years of my life, again and again)

I'm sure during your creation journey, you've experienced one or two of these emotions.

Write down the three coolest things you've ever created:

_____

_____

_____

I believe there could be more emotions, be it a 'Eureka' moment after days of frustration and struggle, or just simply the 'satisfying' 'happy' moment after your creative product is finished.

Let's review these emojis again:

😊😃🤓🤨🤔💤😕☹️🤭🙂😀😅😇😨😠😇😌😐

😂🤣😁😉😎😒😡😔😍🙃😪😦😰😳🥰😗🤗😆

Now, name each of these emojis. I'll start with smile, happy, researching, confusing, question mark, sleepy, wanna give up. Continue on and help me complete the rest.

END

___
___
___

Did you write in English? If you can speak/write in other languages, go back and write down the name of each emoji above in any other language except English.

So, **five years** – Done and dusted! No more!

Yay!!

Yay∞∞∞∞∞∞∞∞∞∞∞∞∞∞∞∞∞∞∞∞∞∞∞∞∞∞∞∞∞∞∞

Wait:

I gradually realised it just continued with more emojis:

as 'creativity' never wants to stop ever since then…

Six years and beyond – my second book *'Infinite (∞) Ways to Stay Creative'* is here (you're reading it), my third, my fourth, my fifth, who knows?

The creativity party has just started, come and join me!

I don't make a living by writing. So it was more than 5 years of effort outside of my full-time work. 5 years? Hell Yeah. You do the math (below)!

5 YEARS

= _____ MONTHS

= _____ DAYS

= _____ HOURS

= _____ MINUTES

= _____ SECONDS

= _____ MILLISECONDS

Wait for a minute, did you just unconsciously fill in the above math questions (or just the top 2 lines, or did you get stuck on converting it to the millisecond)?

But wait for another minute, have you made any assumptions about how much time I actually spent on my book? Did you use those assumptions to calculate the answers to these questions? Put down your assumptions here:

_____   _____

_____   _____

_____   _____

Did you assume that because 1 year has 12 months and 365 days without leap years, 1 day has 24 hours, and 1 hour has 60 minutes, etc, and imagine I was working all that time. Or did you assume that over 5 years I spent 1 or 2 hours outside of work so you assumed 1.5 hours per day over 5 years.

I'm certain that you will come up different assumptions and answers.

END

Have you ever questioned the reason why there are 12 months and 365 days in a year, some months having 31 days, some having only 28 days? Why February has the least number of days? Why can't we have 72 hours per day? And any other questions?

I am sure Google can give you the answers.

Gees, we're going too wild (off the topic) here. Let's get back to my first book production. It sounds like 'painful' and 'time-consuming' work. Why did it take you 5 years? Was it because you're writing too slow? Was it because you're not good enough? Was it because quality work takes time to produce?

Yeah, go on with your questions, as many as possible. I'd say:

- ∞ I was only writing bits and pieces in my spare time.
- ∞ Bright and/or crappy ideas just don't come every day.
- ∞ Life experience helps writing.
- ∞ Artworks add extra work.
- ∞ It was a new experience for me so there was a lot of trial and error for the first book.

If all of this sounds like excuses! I'd say: Don't underestimate the time and effort that is required to create and complete a piece of art. Artwork does require effort and time to develop.

But, don't be scared by the amount of time needed! You don't need 5 years to create something, but if you do something consistently for 5 years, guess what? You become an expert in the field! As you can tell (I bet), how keep writing 5 years has transformed my life, completely. Hey, you wouldn't be holding this book right now without my first 5 years' effort.

During the whole production process, I almost gave up a number of times, I questioned: is publishing a book worth it – financially? I still question that today, even after this book was published. The answer is a **BIG NO** – it's not worth my time and effort or even the money that I put in, sort of. I made a loss, so far.

(Lol, don't be curious about how much an author can make by selling a book. Google can tell you the answer. Instead, be curious on how to create a book yourself, create a piece of music, make a sculpture, draw zentangles, make latte art, plan surprises for people around you, redesign your home – just work on any artwork you'd like.)

But, the whole 'creating' experience is definitely worthwhile, I'd say. That's why I've been keeping going.

See, my creative journey didn't end after publishing my first book. This end is just a new beginning.

And if time permits, I'd just love to continue for a third book, fourth book, fifth book... infinite number of books. Well, to publish an infinite number of books in one's life is a dream, as our time is limited.

The answer is: It's the 'CREATING' process that is a drug to me that I can't get rid of it anymore. Throughout the process, I keep digging out the creative sides of me – different layers, surprising and unexpected! I keep navigating what creativity means, and surprisingly realised that to stay creative, there is an infinite number of ways!

I can't wait to share all these with you!

What are we waiting for? Let's go discover them one by one!

∞ Step Three: Explore **YOUR** magic tools!

Wait, why are we starting from Step Three? Where's Step One and Step Two?

Wow good observation! You've just opened your can of curiosity, and let's get them all out now.

In this chapter, I'm going to give you a number of magic tools to help you stay creative and help you discover your own magic tools. By the end, you'll be able to use these tools to think outside the box.

Not just yet – more amazingly – you'll be able to think both inside and outside a box, or even just on the edge a box, or even for multiple boxes!

What's inside of the box? Chocolates, books, 'I love you' signs, French macarons, Olympic medals, air, ocean, surprises, nothing? What's outside of the box then?

Wait, why 'think outside the box' only – why not 'outside the gift box, shoe box, gogglebox'?

What is the material of these boxes? Carton, paper, metal, plastic, steel, aluminium, polymer, leather, textile, glass, ceramics, wood, foam, ceramic, gold, diamond, you name it.

Gather your magic tools

First of all first, straight to the topic — let's gather some magic tools that help you with your creative journeys along the way, which are listed in the below:

- ∞ a car
- ∞ alcohol
- ∞ a pen
- ∞ a laptop
- ∞ multiple pieces of paper
- ∞ a lighter (optional)
- ∞ a bathroom
- ∞ a treadmill
- ∞ books
- ∞ a smart phone?
- ∞ a powerful mind
- ∞ an AI tool
- ∞ a notebook
- ∞ highlighters

Do you really need all these tools? Cross out the ones that you think are useless.

As you go through the book, look for these tools, use them in your next project design, then add new tools as you explore the book.

Or, maybe I even didn't mention some of the tools above in the book at all.

Next activities: draw a cute picture after each tool above and colour them any way you like — see where it takes your brain.

Hope your creativity has taken off from this moment onwards. 66, the number of this topic, is a lucky number in Chinese, so you're starting off with luck! Good luck!

Step Three: Explore YOUR magic tools!

Start with a definition

When starting your new project, new product, artwork, giving it a definition helps to get your audience's attention and gives them an understanding of what you'll be talking about.

Since we are talking about the 'creative' throughout the book, let's give a definition of creativity. What does it mean to you? Put it down on the blank areas below.

_____

_____

_____

There could just be thousands of ways to describe being creative. Here are my suggestions:

- ∞ Creativity is something that you use to make something.
- ∞ Creativity is to '**cre**ate' '**any**' 'ac**tivity**'.
- ∞ Creativity is when your ideas spark, when you find one of the best ways to solve a problem, when you figure out or invent something that others haven't done so.
- ∞ Creativity is a mindset that most people don't think they possess, but it's an awesome unique creative nature that everyone is born with.

Creativity is a creation process from nothing to something amazing, to something out of this world!

There are no silly suggestions. Yours are unique, and ours are compatible but not comparable.

Now let's give a definition of the word 'Infinite' in the book title. What does it mean to you?

Limitation is/isn't a limitation

Green Eggs & Ham, a bestselling children's book, was written by Dr. Seuss back in 1960. What's unique about this book? Dr. Seuss's editor bet him that he couldn't write the entire book only using 50 words.

Result? Dr. Seuss accepted the challenge and wrote his book which went on to be a best-seller.

Wow!

Setting up constraints can boost your creativity level.

These constraints are also designed to limit you. However, you can use them to activate your brain cells so you can break through these limitations in other ways in the end.

Agree?

Now challenge yourself to:
- ∞ do something for 7 days in a row
- ∞ complete a poem in 20 seconds
- ∞ use one stroke to draw anything
- ∞ draw circles for 1 minute – as many as you can.

What challenges will you set up for yourself for your next project?

Step Three: Explore YOUR magic tools!

Make math your favourite subject

Isn't math amazing? No, it isn't. It's super amazing!

Math exists in mother nature:

- ∞ Hexagons are found in _____.

- ∞ Concentric circles are found in _____.

- ∞ Golden ratio (approximately equal to 1.618) is found in _____.

Give your answers in above blank spaces, or pick one or few from the following:

> Beehive, ideal human body proportions, snowflakes, ripples of a pond when throwing a stone in.

Have you realised that math functions and formulas are super-magical and can be applied almost in every aspect in our real life?

- ∞ creativity = 100% of practice + 1000% of your natural talent
- ∞ sour + sweet + bitter + spicy = life
- ∞ family > work

Do you agree with above formulas that I made up? Some people find formulas make more sense than a written saying such as 'Family should always come first. Work can be second'.

Now, I need to borrow your creativity to help me complete the two formulas below.

∞ _____ x _____ x _____ = happiness

∞ (_____ + _____ + _____)^2 - _____ = success

Step Three: Explore YOUR magic tools!

Decode 'From' and 'To'

The words 'From' and 'To' are wonderful and powerful, which gives us directions, ranges, possibilities on what can be done, should be done or what can't. Examples include:

from A to Z

from left to right

from head to toe

from top to bottom

from home to work

from zero to infinite

from rookie to pro

from credit to debit

from the ancient to the modern world

from the beginning to the end

from hometown to all round the world

We can expand even further – from A to B to C to Z to ZZ, from left to top left to the right to the bottom right, from the beginning to 20% to 50% to the end to a new beginning. You get the gist, right? During this process, you should've drawn multiple directions, ranges and possibilities in your mind, on paper, or using software. There are infinite directions, ranges and possibilities!

Google is a great assistant, indeed.

On 20 July 2022, in the early morning, I sat down, in front of my laptop. I had no idea where to start to write about creativity.

Alright, I will google, I thought. Google will have an answer. I started typing *is writing*…in the Google search bar. Guess what? I was instantly inspired by the responses that emerged from this random question.

- ∞ Is writing on your hand bad?
- ∞ Is writing art?
- ∞ Is writing better than typing?
- ∞ Is writing notes a wasting of time?
- ∞ Is writing non-verbal communication?
- ∞ Is writing a gross motor skill?
- ∞ Is writing on your skin bad?
- ∞ Is writing in red rude?

It's been an awesome start. I then typed *Does writing*… Guess what I got?

- ∞ Does writing notes actually help?
- ∞ Does writing help you remember?
- ∞ Does writing help retain information?
- ∞ Does writing notes help memory?
- ∞ Does writing in color improve memory?
- ∞ Does writing burn calories?
- ∞ Does writing in a journal help?
- ∞ Does writing icing set hard?
- ∞ Does wiring make you smarter?
- ∞ Does writing books make money?
- ∞ Does writing cause frustration from time to time?

Step Three: Explore YOUR magic tools!

Does writing burn calories? Wow, I like this brilliant (one zillion dollar) question – the best! With curiosity, I clicked into a few websites, the answer is: yes, we burn calories while writing, but it's only to a certain extent, which isn't enough for us to lose weight. No wonder I didn't lose weight with intensive writing!

Now my brain is activated, I start to question:

- ∞ Does writing make you fat?
- ∞ Does writing heal a broken heart?
- ∞ Why do we human beings write?
- ∞ What should we write?
- ∞ Where to write?
- ∞ …

Now my brain moves to somewhere else, and it's unstoppable! Suddenly I'm in the writing flow, and it's hard to stop me.

Infinite Ways to Stay Creative

Look for a pattern

Can you memorise these numbers in just 10 seconds?

365412527246031400

Let's look for a pattern here: 365 (days in a year) 4 (quarters in a year) 12 (months in a year) 52 (weeks in a year) 7 (days in a week) 24 (hours in a day) 60 (minutes in an hour) 314 (an apple 'pie') 00 (our infinite symbol when they're close friends). Does the task become easier now?

Now let's look for a similarity/dissimilarity between something. List all types of bosses that you've encountered or heard of across your career. I'll give you examples and add more in the blank area.

caring, sharp, sweet, smart, real leader, inspiring, listen, accountable	VS	stupid, toxic, asshole, takes the credit for other's work, ducks responsibility, micromanages

Conclusion? Looking for a pattern helps us summarise things quickly and better, and solve problems creatively. Let's practise one more looking for a pattern activity – fill in the next four numbers in the blank.

1, 1, 2, 3, 5, 8, __, __, __, __

What you've filled in is called Fibonacci sequence. These numbers are called Fibonacci numbers, so the first ten Fibonacci numbers are 1,1,2,3,5,8,13,21,34,55. Did you get it right easily?

Step Three: Explore YOUR magic tools!

Ask questions like [   ]

Why are there square brackets [   ] in the title?

I'm glad you've just asked a question with your curious mind. I'd like you to use your imagination to add something inside each set of brackets below to make the title more vivid.

Ask questions like what or like who, like a kid, like you know nothing, like whenever whatever you like. There are never stupid questions. By asking questions like [   ], you're navigating your thoughts, gaining knowledge, exploring all possibilities and creative solutions, getting to your answers eventually.

Now ask questions, any, creativity related or not related. Let me get started:

- ∞ Why is there a running app called Strava?
- ∞ What's a digital candle made of?
- ∞ Which book should never have been written?
- ∞ What will next century look like?
- ∞ Why did you crack open this book?
- ∞ Do I really want to be a creative person?

Let me have some wild guesses on the second last question:

- ∞ I saw someone reading the book in a café, in a train, in the waiting area at the airport, at the library, in the botanic gardens.

- ∞ Curiosity led me here by checking up the 'what-the-hell' on the book cover.
- ∞ I got the book as a door gift from company's event.
- ∞ I randomly searched 'best sellers' on Amazon and liked the reviews.

For the last question above, you might find your own answers in the section titled: 'Step Two: Upgrade YOUR thinking!'

The magic tool of 'ask questions like [   ]' is now all yours.

It's your turn to 'ask questions like [   ]'.

Step Three: Explore YOUR magic tools!

5Ws and 2Hs

You might have already noticed, to ask questions like [   ], **5Ws and 2Hs** are here to help.

Let's take a look at the following questions:

- ∞ **Why do we say 'curiosity kills a cat'?** It's a proverb.
- ∞ **Who said 'Curiosity kills a cat'?** Ben Johnson.
- ∞ **When did Ben say this?** In 1598.
- ∞ **Where?** In Ben Johnson's play. He wrote, 'Care killed that cat'.
- ∞ **What killed a cat?** Care.
- ∞ **How come 'care killed a cat' in 1598?** Care meant 'worry' back then.
- ∞ **Have you noticed that we have used '5Ws and 2Hs' tool to ask questions?** Yes.
- ∞ **Do we still need the curiosity?** Yes.
- ∞ **Isn't this too cruel if 'curiosity does kill a cat'?** Yes.
- ∞ **Are you with me?** Yes.
- ∞ **Should we potentially upgrade the name of the tool to '5Ws, 2Hs and 1D-I-A-S'?** Yes.
- ∞ **Or, potentially, the name would be extended further?** Yes.

Well done! The '5Ws and 2Hs' is an abbreviated version which can easily remind us that we can always grab this magic tool as we please – '5Ws and 2Hs', to explore all possibilities and boost our creativity.

Now, let's ask more questions, any. Drop down your one-million-dollar questions in the blank wavy lines.

- ∞ Who created the alphabet?
- ∞ Observe tennis trophy images, why does it pose like that?
- ∞ How about living a day without digital distractions?
- ∞ Where does the name iPhone come from?
- ∞ Why are you doing what you're doing?
- ∞ _____
- ∞ _____

Step Three: Explore YOUR magic tools!

What if?

Continue on with Topic 59 and 58, ask as many 'what-if?' questions as possible. It could lead you nowhere, somewhere, anywhere, or everywhere.

- ∞ What if Vincent van Gogh sold all his paintings and made a decent income when he was alive, maybe he would not have committed suicide?
- ∞ What if there was no gravity?
- ∞ What if you could change one thing in history, what would you change?
- ∞ What if you have a 'pause' button to stop time?
- ∞ What if you're Elon Musk?

List your 'what if' questions down below, as many as possible. Go wild!

Draw out your mind map

Let's run a brainstorming session together. I've listed a few things that we might have or will experience for the first time in our life, and help me grow the list:

- ∞ walk
- ∞ go to school
- ∞ graduate
- ∞ fall in love
- ∞ get married
- ∞ no longer care what others think of me
- ∞ grow grey hair
- ∞ _____
- ∞ _____
- ∞ _____
- ∞ _____

Now running out all ideas?

Don't worry. Your mind map is here to help – a magic technique to brainstorm and explore all possibilities. Sometimes, once you've started one or two ideas, the rest magically flows through one by one.

Now take out a large piece of paper. Put down 'first time in my life' in the centre, then use your exercise brain, chemistry brain, musical brain, logical brain, left brain, right brain…keep branching it out further. Think of all the things you have done for a first time in your life. Give it a wild go! The map looks prettier, delivering messages faster and clearer than if they were put in a list like the one above.

Step Three: Explore YOUR magic tools!

Do you agree?

For those who haven't heard of a mind map, I drew an example below for 'My New Year's resolutions'. Any shapes, any colours, any designs are really at your choice, and you're making a beautiful piece of art while generating millions of ideas. How cool is it!

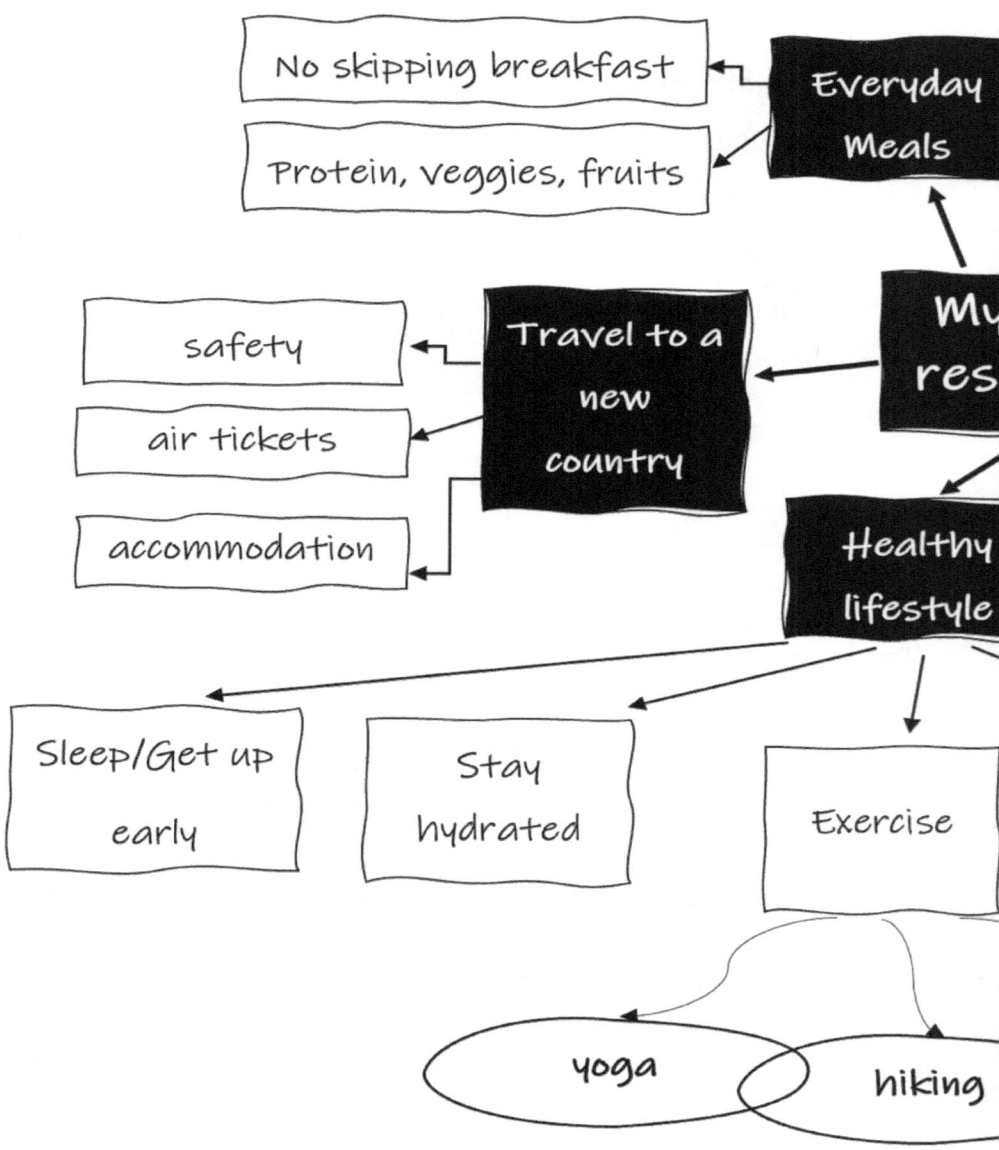

I drew my mind map using Microsoft Word software. There are heaps of mind mapping tools and templates available online, which are free for you to grab! Just google it!

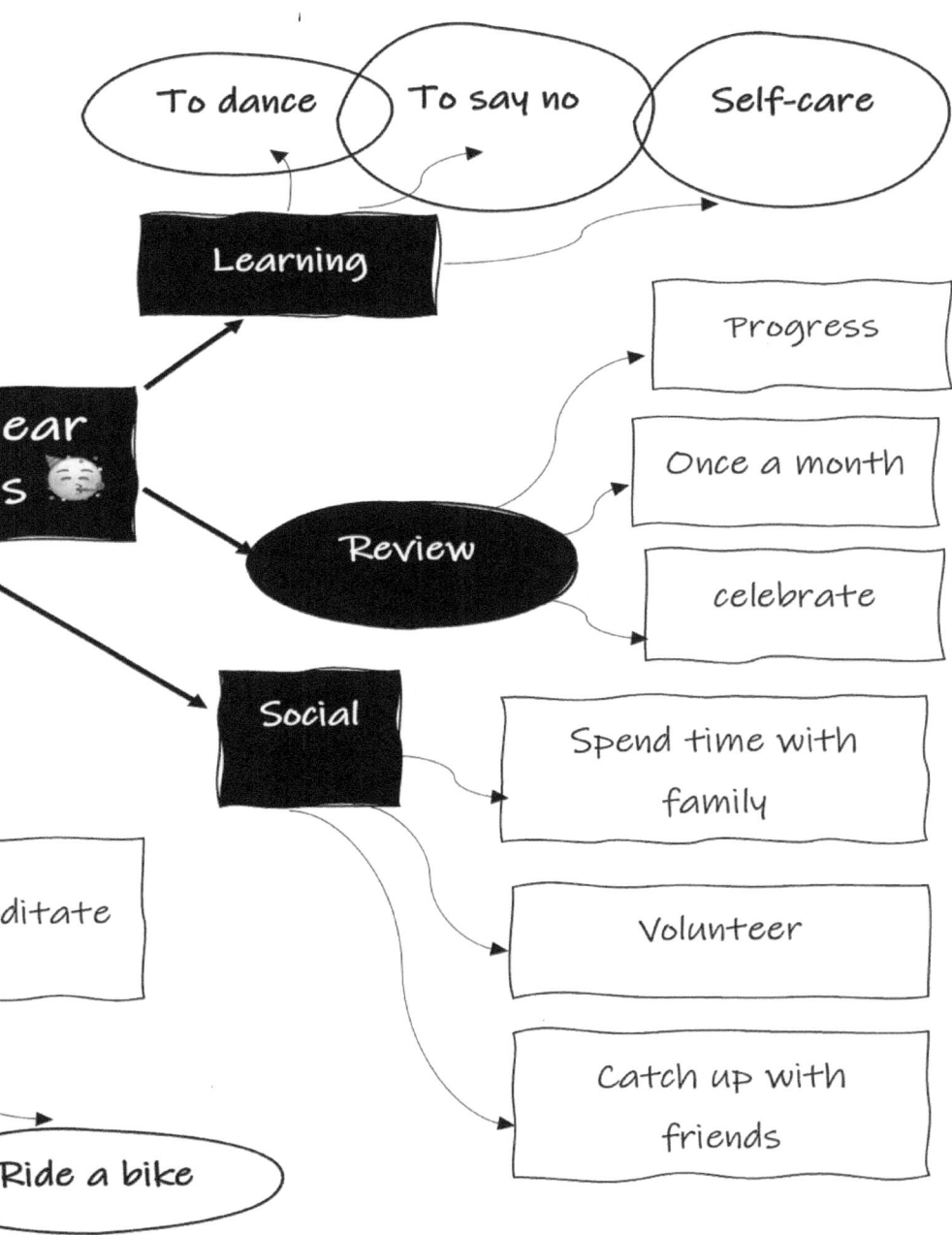

Step Three: Explore YOUR magic tools!

Tell me stories, please!

One day, a girl was drawing at class, the teacher asked: 'What are you drawing?' 'I'm drawing a picture of God.' 'How would you know what God looks like as no one knows!' The little girl answered, 'They will in a minute.'

I heard this story in a TED talk by Sir Ken Robinson. I have adopted this idea now and you can too. I'll tell this story when I talk about 'why we shouldn't be afraid of being wrong.'

Talking about **peer pressure**? Well, I believe the peer pressure exists in the real world. Boring and unconvincing?

An experiment, called the Asch Conformity Test, was conducted in the 1950s. It was designed to test peer pressure in decision making. Questions were asked such as 'which line on the right-hand side card is the same length as the line on the left-hand card.'

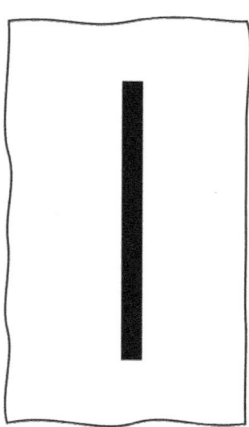
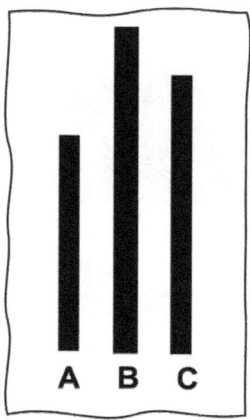

A participant was led into the room with a group of actors. The participant was not aware they were actors nor that they had been told to give predefined answers. The experiment found that the group of actors could influence the answers of the participants because when no actors were present almost all participants were able to give the correct answer. But when the actors were present, the participants often mimicked the actors and gave the wrong answers. Wow, the power of the peer pressure!

I also would like to tell you a story that shows that sometimes it is really important to disregard other's opinions! A long time ago, when the first dentist proposed people should brush their teeth twice a day to protect against germs, people laughed at the idea, and no one believed them! Looking us now, I bet most people brush their teeth twice a day.

I noticed that bestselling books have interesting and convincing stories in them. *The Art of Creative Thinking: 89 Ways to See Things Differently* by Rod Judkins is one of those. (Oops, should I upgrade '*Infinite (∞) Ways to Stay Creative*' to be a book full of stories and make it a best-seller?)

Anyone can be a story-teller whether it's your story or others, theirs, mine, or a combination of all of them. You can draw people into your story and inspire them, so have a go and write one down.

Step Three: Explore YOUR magic tools!

Bring it on – interesting principles, laws, theories...

To make your stories more vivid, consider adding interesting principles, laws, theories, or even defining some 'random' numbers into your stories to help grab your audience's attention. Below are 16 interesting principles, laws, theories, effects, methods, or syndromes. How many have you heard of?

Butterfly	Birdcage	Buckets	Snowball
Broken windows	Splitting hairs	Stockholm	Ripple
Domino	Pareto	Zero-sum	6-3-5
Let them	Murphy's	Laurence J. Peter	Always

I really like the 6-5-3 method – **six** people in a group, spending **five** minutes, to come up with **three** ideas on a piece of paper. Once the time is up, pass the piece of paper to the person on your right. Then repeat the process until the first piece of paper comes back to you. This is a brainstorming technique, originally published by Bernd Rohrbach in a German sales magazine in 1968.

In the table above, either draw the animal or object in the square or place a tick next to a person's name.

All of these are drawn from real-life experiences, so you can create these principles, laws, theories, effects, methods, or syndromes, based on your own real-life experiences, seriously! I could give you a few: compound interest rate principle, start right now principle, writing addiction syndrome, 3-2-1 method, etc.

Infinite Ways to Stay Creative

Say hello to charts and graphs

When you'd like to produce something impressive and eye-catching, don't forget visual presentations – charts and graphs! They speak louder than words. Agreed?

Below are two charts I created. Do these charts tell you stories, even though the data is made up! There's also line chart, scatter chart, bubble chart, 3D area chart, waterfall chart, ribbon chart, table chart, combo of these charts, etc. Use them wherever applicable.

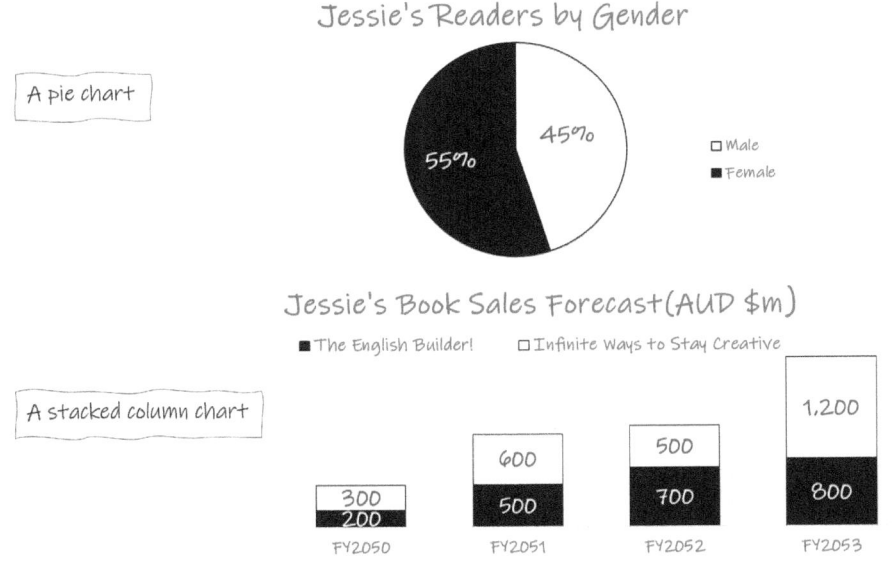

Here are the rules to consider in your chart design:

- ∞ Fancy formatting can be overwhelming, so the simpler and cleaner the better.
- ∞ Avoid using **red** and **green** colours in one graph to make it color-blind friendly.
- ∞ When there are more than five elements don't use a pie chart, it will get too busy.
- ∞

Step Three: Explore YOUR magic tools!

Shapes and colors are your choice

There are around 500 million shapes and over 10 million colours in the world. WOW!

Shapes are two-dimensional, having a length and width. They help to create complex drawings and are everywhere in our daily life. Using different shapes as symbols to list items, gives the reader a fresh view. Like below:

Hey, numbers are also shapes, aren't they? We can make these **adorable shapes** into different sizes, change their angle, color them... There are infinite illustrations for you to use!

This page is referring to 10 million colors existing in the world, but they are only in black and white. Now take out your markers, highlighters, crayons, colour

Did your eyes and attentions come here when flicking through this page? Adding a note sticker in your project can successfully grab your audience's attention.

pencils, watercolor brushes, or whatever tools you have available to make the shapes below unique and vivid.

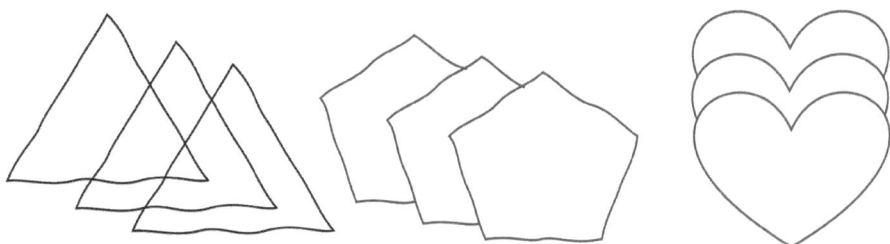

Did you pay particular attention to the sticky note (**a shape**), the **bold and big** words on the page? Yeah, they're just brilliant ways to get attention.

Step Three: Explore YOUR magic tools!

Art in different forms

MasterChef Australia is my favourite cooking show. One thing that once inspired me was when a contestant cooked an ingredient in a variety of different ways (say fried mushrooms, hibachi mushrooms, roasted mushrooms) in one dish. As a result, that dish was super-tasty and highly rated by the judges. Wow, what an innovative way to do things, to add the layers and variety to it!

How about presenting Eiffel Tower in three ways? See below!

My artwork - paint by number

My artwork – photography

My artwork – scratch postcard

Question: What other ways that you can also present the Eiffel Tower?

Conclusion: Art and things can be presented in so many forms. Use the tools you have available and do one thing in different forms, as many as possible! See where does this practice take you?

Infinite Ways to Stay Creative

Make it sharp and sweet

For any products you're making or services to promote, all you need to do is get your ideas across, sharp and sweet. Just like how I'm doing it right now on this page.

Draw potential tools that you'll need in the blank area below:

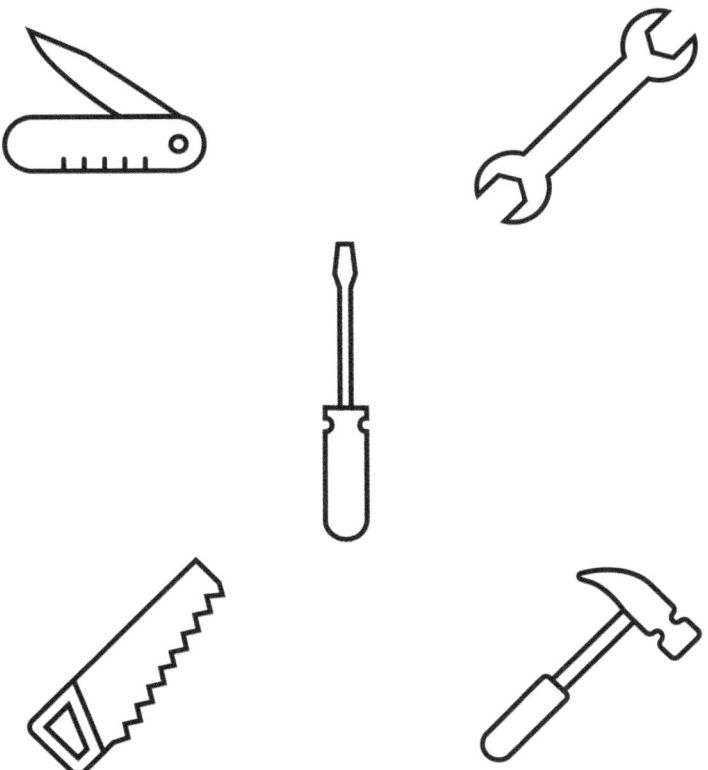

Step Three: Explore YOUR magic tools!

Magic tools – A LOT – INFINITE, basically!

I'm going to hand over the secret sauce here: magic tools for your creative projects or interesting ideas are out there, both in your home, out there in the nature, anywhere in the world – a lot. Basically, anything could become your magic tool – Infinite!

Don't believe me? I'll give you a few examples:

- ∞ From **an apple**, Newton created Newton's law.
- ∞ **Winds** are used for power generation.
- ∞ With **pens and brushes**, world-renowned paintings have been created.
- ∞ **Adobe Creative** design software has helped produce zillions of artworks.
- ∞ Your **mobile phone** is a great tool for taking photos or videos.
- ∞ **AI** (Artificial Intelligence) can produce 50K words for a book within a day. (Are human writers still needed?)
- ∞ _____
- ∞ _____

Add in your own examples in the wavy line above.

No tool is a one-of-a-kind magic tool. Simply let your mind do the wondering. When your mind drifts, you come to a place that's full of imagination and possibilities. We need those spaces and those moments. I come to those places when I:

- ∞ observe a bunch of **ants** crawling
- ∞ have **radio** on while driving (a **car**)

- ∞ daydream (**my brain**)
- ∞ gardening (**flowers, trees, water** and **garden tools**).

These are examples of my own magic tools. I have an infinite number of them! You have an infinite number of them too! Find these magic tools and let them do wonders for you, fit them to your own purpose, use them, and use them well – to communicate your brilliant artwork or your brilliant ideas out to the world. The sky is your limit. No, the sky isn't your limit.

∞ Step Two: Upgrade **YOUR** thinking!

In this chapter, we will train ourselves to form a new way of thinking (not a stereotype), and it's our own unique way of thinking. You'll be inspired to find infinite ways to improve your artwork, your creative craft and any problems surfacing in your life.

Don't believe me?

Well, if you don't continue to read through, how would you know if I'm wasting your time or giving you the mindset your creative nature needs?

Worth giving it a try?

Well, let's start with answering this question: What is your current relationship with creativity?

- [ ] I couldn't bother.
- [ ] He/she (or It) is a stranger.
- [ ] We used to be close friends, but not anymore.
- [ ] We're nurturing each other.
- [ ] Our relationship has ever grown stronger and stronger.

Creativity is everyone's birthright – no kidding.

You brain is a super amazing organ. You become what you think, you become what you believe. I think Elizabeth Gilbert agreed with me as she once said, 'If you're alive, you are a creative person.' (Oops, it might be me agreeing with her.)

Here are some quotes about 'being creative':

> 'You can't use up creativity. The more you use, the more you have.'
> **– Maya Angelou**

> 'Creativity involves breaking out of expected patterns in order to look at things in a different way.'
> **– Edward de Bono**

> 'If you want creative workers, give them enough time to play.'
> **– John Cleese**

> 'Creativity is inventing, experimenting, growing, taking risks, breaking rules, making mistakes, and having fun.'
> **– Mary Lou Cook**

> 'Creativity can solve almost any problem. The creative act, the defeat of habit by originality, overcomes everything.'
> **– George Lois**

Now it's your turn. Make your own original quote for the day. Make it **bold**, and in the biggest font size on the page. Write it down and then post it onto all your social media platforms. (How many platforms do you have?)

Step Two: Upgrade YOUR thinking!

I agree with all the above quotes, maybe even yours. But you shouldn't just read them for the sake of reading them, or write it for the sake of writing it.

One day, your quote might go viral on the internet, you might become a celebrity, or you might already be one. Who knows? One more question: Do you know any of the above-mentioned people I quoted? Are they famous? Are they all legends?

You are a creative genius!

Adding onto Topic 48, I'm saying again that 'Everyone is a creative genius, yes, yourself and I are both included, everyone is included.' Buddha assures you that you become who you think you are. You are creative and a genius! And indeed you're.

Tell me what is the most creative and crazy thing that you've done so far in life. What's the second most creative stuff you've done, third, fourth, and so on.

Step Two: Upgrade YOUR thinking!

What can you do with your creativity?

Since you've upgraded your thinking to believe that each of you is a creative genius, what can you do with your creativity? To what extent? Drastically, dramatically, surprisingly, quietly, loudly, creatively…Follow the patterns below, and add your creativity thinking.

Increase your creativity

Boost your creativity

> What the hell of this is? I can't read it, me either. Well, give a guess.

Develop your creativity

Improve your creativity

Do something about it

Just do creatively

Create creatively

Make creatively

Write creatively

Think creatively

Create creativity in your day job

Excuse me? I'm not an artist, a musician, a writer, a designer, or a PHD student studying human being's creativity. How am I supposed to be 'creative' daily?

What if I tell you that every profession is creative, mentally, physically, spiritually?

Let me give you an example.

I'm an accountant.

Hey, accountants are just number crunchers all day long. Nope, don't let the stereotype get you. Even if I'm just crunching numbers, I'd do it in a fun and creative way. How?

At the start of my career, I spent most of my day job entering invoices – dull and boring? Then I treated 'hitting the keyboard' is a chance for creation, different strokes, different rhythms – listen carefully, I'm making many pieces of music every day, basically.

As time goes by, I've become an Excel pro. Wow, I just absolutely love this magic tool for my creativity work! An Excel sheet is my canvas; I've created countless professional dashboards and automated and streamlined processes just on this blank canvas.

Now, spiritually – professionally, I'm now an accounting, finance and IT artist.

It's your time to shine, creative genius, you can make your everyday job a creative one as well. From now on, your relationship with creativity is every day, and you can't get rid of the word from your life anymore, that is, **CREATIVITY**!

Step Two: Upgrade YOUR thinking!

You are a fabulous creative artist

What's the relationship between creativity and making art? Do you agree with the illustration below?

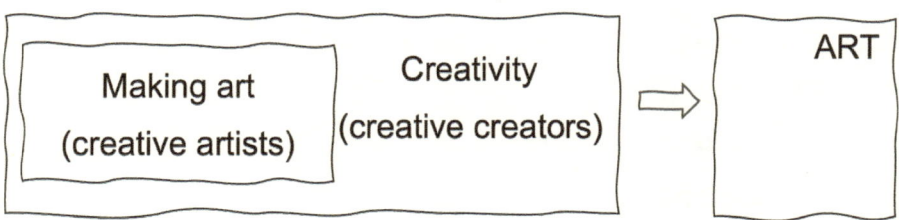

I'd like to feed you the following mindset. You need to label yourself and reinforce it into your brain that you're a fabulous, creative artist.

Lots of people just don't have the courage to give themselves the title 'artist', as they don't believe they are. But they actually are. Let me give you a few examples below:

I work in accounting. I'm a fabulous creative accountant-artist.

I work in teaching. I'm a fabulous creative teacher-artist.

I work in the arts. I'm a fabulous creative art-artist.

I play basketball. I'm a fabulous creative basketball-artist.

I do the laundry. I'm a fabulous creative laundry-artist.

I play Teris, I'm a fabulous creative Teris-artist.

Whatever you do, you're a fabulous creative artist.

Anything you do is ART

If you agree with what I said in Topic 44 that you're a **fabulous creative artist,** then you'd agree that 'Anything you do, is **ART.**'

From small decisions on what to wear, what to eat, to completing a billion-dollar creative project, you're forever innovative. When you do, what you do, how you do it is art in your own unique way.

For example, the way you start your day is art. Making your bed is art; not making your bed is also art – even though I would highly recommend starting your day by making your bed, which brings you luck and success for the day as well as your creativity project. Don't believe me? Try it!

How you're reading this book right now, and how your brain processes these related or non-related words is also art.

Step Two: Upgrade YOUR thinking!

Upgrade your mindset, as a fabulous creative artist

Hello, fabulous creative artist, from now on, I need you to **upgrade your mindset,** which is everything, which is powerful.

Here's a story:

Two men A and B went to sell shoes in a village, and both noticed that no one wore shoes in this village.

Salesman A got a conclusion: everyone in the village is barefoot. They don't need a pair of shoes at all.

Salesman B also got a conclusion: everyone in the village is barefoot. It's a great opportunity to sell the shoes to everyone.

Guess which salesman could sell his shoes — A or B?

Here's another trick: when something bad happens, we usually react by thinking negatively, question why me? It affects our mood, then more bad things follow! This leads us into a downward spiral which seems as if it's never ending. Instead, I want you to upgrade your mindset – think in an opposite direction.

Let's put it into practice:

One morning my usual train to work was cancelled; passengers were asked to take a bus to another train station, which took me an extra hour to get to work.

What a morning! Well, it wasn't too bad. I got the chance to experience something new, a 'free' bus tour in a suburb that I wouldn't normally visit. It wasn't 'another bland and boring day' that I'd forget easily. It's a day that's quite impressive. With that morning's little surprise, I'm now telling you this story in my book, to raise your awareness of 'upgrade your mindset'. See, things do happen for a reason.

Age isn't just a number

I like the quote: 'Age is just a number.'

But I also firmly believe 'Age isn't just a number – it's a symbol of wisdom. As you grow, wisdom grows.' It makes perfect sense that 'you're never too late to start anything.' Instead, starting something in your adulthood helps you better understand things, possibly producing more valuable more creative work.

So age is no barrier – the only barrier is the limitation of your mind.

Step Two: Upgrade YOUR thinking!

Present lousy excuses = Future massive regrets

Let's keep below formula in mind all the time:

> **Present lousy excuses = Future massive regrets**

What are excuses? Excuses are excuses. They're your future massive regrets, and they're lousy:

- ∞ born and raised in a poor family — I'll never become wealthy
- ∞ work is super busy — so I don't have time for any other things
- ∞ weather is horrible — so I'll go to gym tomorrow
- ∞ it's so much trouble to plan a holiday — so I give up.

These are so classic.

You're just being creative with your excuses, but not being creative with finding solutions and taking action.

Looking back years later, you'd realise that opportunities were missed, and you've never had a go at things you'd like to try. Start to question why you made so many lousy excuses for not doing things many years ago.

So, next time when you're battling with your lousy excuses, keep this formula in mind as well:

> **Future NO regrets = Present NO excuses**

Words have their power

Words do have their power – super power. Positive language attracts positive outcomes and artworks. Negativity can only bring you crap in the end.

Imagine when you're angry, when you're feeling blue, when you have so many negativities, do you still have any happy space in your brain to create something creative? I bet it's a no.

How do the words below make you feel?

Adventurous	Blessing	Confident	Delightful	Endearing	Flourish
Glow	Harmony	Inspired	Joy	Kindness	Lucky
Motivated	Neat	Optimal	Peaceful	Quiet	Relaxed
Stellar	Thrilled	Upbeat	Vibrant	Winning	Xoompin
Yay	Zappy				

What about the words below?

Anxious	Brutal	Conflict	Dirty	Endanger	Foolish
Glitch	Harassed	Insulting	Jeopardise	Killjoy	Loser
Misuse	Nightmare	Obstacle	Punish	Quitter	Racist
Suffer	Toxic	Unsecure	Violent	Weak	Xenophobia
Yuck	Zombie				

Did the first table make you happy and energetic while the second table make you unmotivated or annoyed?

This is the power of words. From this moment on, delete boring dumb negative words in your vocabulary. Surround yourself with super powerful words and fellow creators who have a positive mindset. If we all do this, what would be the world look like?

Step Two: Upgrade YOUR thinking!

Is what you see what you see?

Hey, the fabulous creative artist, what do you see in the picture below?

Did you see a mobile phone?

Think it again. Let me know what you saw.

Well, I see a mobile, a screen, my iPhone, good memories in my photos, work emails, Apple store, next generation iPhone release, phone manufacturing work environment, Modern Slavery Act. How can I survive a day in my life without it...the list just goes on, goes on, and goes on.

Well, I've just been rejected for a job opportunity. What did you see? Being rejected? No. I'd see myself getting an even better job offer in another month. Bye, this one! Next, please!

Well, the trick here is what you see isn't always what you see, see further, see forward, upward, downward, backward, 30-degree, 60-degree, 360-degree or even 720-degree, see the unsee.

Infinite Ways to Stay Creative

720-degree thinking strategy

Let's start with an interesting activity. Draw below masterpiece on a piece of blank A4 paper without lifting your pen throughout. Are you able to make it?

I encourage you to think 720 degrees for exam questions, work problems, family relations, or whatever happens in life. 720 degrees is greater than 360 degrees. It's not just one circle, it's moving circles (not static), which means we need to:

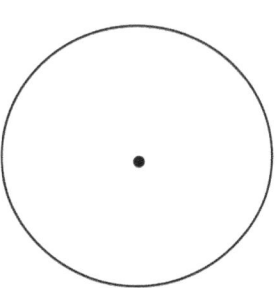

- ∞ peel away the different layers, all layers
- ∞ look at things from multiple perspectives
- ∞ have a 'helicopter' or big picture view
- ∞ play the long game and move forward.

All good things will follow through, naturally.

Have you worked out the above question using 720-degree thinking methodology?

Well, after drawing the little dot, lift up one corner of the paper, fold it to where your pen stays, draw a line then a circle! Go complete it in the illustration to the right.

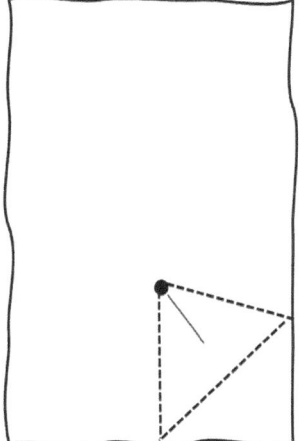

Next question: how can you add another circle to get 720 degrees for us without lifting your pen?

Step Two: Upgrade YOUR thinking!

There's never a setback

Hey there, little creators, do you know setbacks will hit your door at some stage in life, if they haven't yet. Setbacks suck! You may feel as if the whole world is dark, falling and against you?

However, the creative genius, have you ever thought maybe they are not a setback at all? It's just a step for us to move upward, getting something even better in the end. So should we call it 'step-up' moving forward, though each of us could experience different steps, different timeframes, a different number of 'step-ups'. The graphs below show some examples:

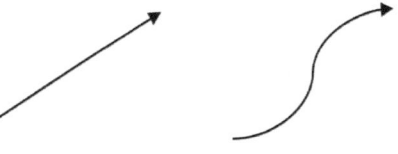

Give 'step-ups' another name that you think most suitable and draw a couple of your 'step-ups' path in the blank area below.

> This line could end up surging up to other pages, or out of the book, or even out of the world. Who knows?

When things do not go your way, use this 'bad to good to marvellous' mindset:

Bad: When I caught Covid in 2023, I lost my sense of smell, taste and interest in anything. I found myself reaching the point of depression for the first time in my life.

To Good: Two months after catching Covid, I got a new job offer just 6 weeks after starting to search for opportunities. How do these two events relate? Well, I'm a big believer that 'misfortune leads to even better fortune.'

To Marvellous: I still suffer from long covid today with brain fog from time to time. But this experience has made me realise people with depression suffer a lot. So I've joined the Melbourne annual 2XU – Go Beyond Blue running event twice to raise people's awareness of the importance of mental health and physical activity. (Hey, are you aware that staying creative also brings joy and lowers your stress hormones?)

When I come across 'step-ups', I jump and bounce better and stronger. As someone once said, 'What doesn't kill you makes you stronger.' Who's that someone?

Step Two: Upgrade YOUR thinking!

Break your brain's biases

There are a lot of interesting unconscious biases existing in our brain, which could limit your beliefs and impact your decision-making.

Try below three questions:

Question 1: **1% fat** yogurt vs. **99% fat free** yogurt, which yogurt are you going to buy?

Question 2: Young people are good with technology. True or False?

Question 3: I had a meal at Biases restaurant (it was my first visit), which left me with an upset stomach two days later. Would I go back to that Biases restaurant again?

Now put your thinking cap on – what are below biases and give one example for each.

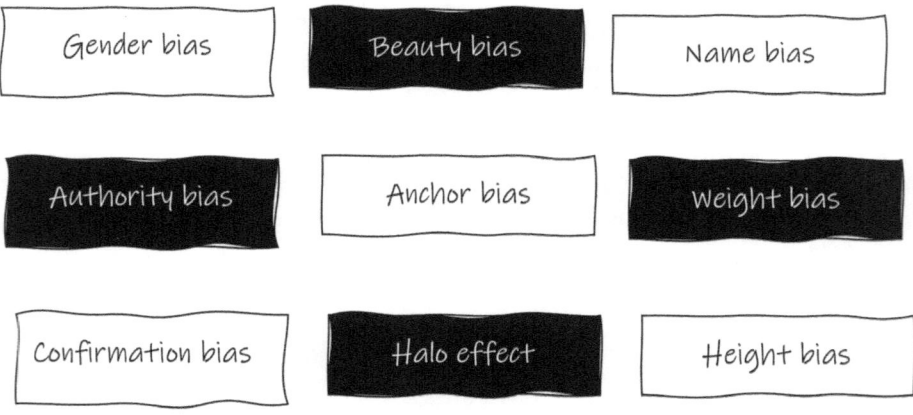

What should we do about our biases? Identify them, assess them, keep them, ditch them, beat them, break them, overcome them? What would you like to do with them?

You're right, but never assume you're right

We, as human beings, often:

- ∞ don't like conflict, different opinions or being criticised
- ∞ assume that what we say or what we do are always right
- ∞ find it hard to accept that we're in the wrong.

Yes, you're right, no matter if you realise you're 100% right, 50% of right or 0% right, in hindsight.

But, we, as human being creators, we should learn to embrace this colourful, dynamic and amazing world, understand that each of our fellow creators' ideas are original because of their genes, beliefs, knowledge and experience. We're all unique in our own way.

So, we, as human being creators, should be aware and often reflect:

- ∞ conflict, different views or critics adds new and interesting perspectives on our beliefs
- ∞ maybe we should accept the idea that we never agree with, and give it a go
- ∞ we can't be absolutely right all the time, though we don't like admitting it.

So, whatever (feedback, advice, suggestion) others give you, treat it as a birthday gift. Appreciate it. But if you don't like it, you can just quietly throw it into the bin. It doesn't matter.

What matters is never doubt yourself, regardless of whether you're right or not right. You're always the most shining, stunning, amazing, brilliant and fabulous creative artist!

Step Two: Upgrade YOUR thinking!

Your money can be your best friend

Money isn't everything.

I'd like to encourage you to change that mindset to: 'Money is important and could be your best friend forever and ever.'

Imagine your life without your best friend – you won't be able to pay your rent/mortgage, your bills and your meals – then how come you have the mood to work on your brilliant, creative ideas that could potentially bring you a fortune?

So put your blood and sweat into your day job (don't quit it just because you don't like it – remember to use the 720-degree strategy to see things!), your artwork, your creative ideas or hobbies outside of your day job at the same time.

Be in awe of money, and use it wisely. But, keep the formula below in mind:

Your money

= Your best friend forever and ever

Infinite Ways to Stay Creative

Appreciate the beauty of imperfection

How do the four pictures below make you feel?

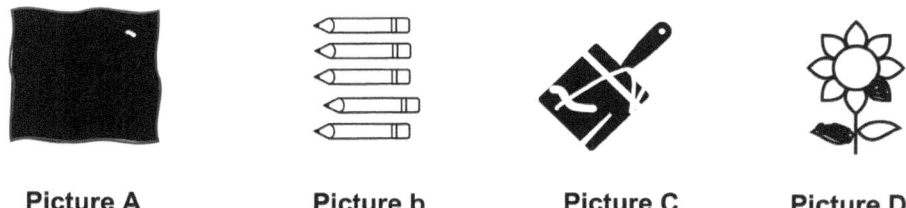

The **white dot** must be filled in picture A.

The **letter b** in the title needs to be capitalised. Move **the fourth pencil** forward a bit.

Has a naughty kid **destroyed** picture C?

Colour in **all** the flower petals and leaves in picture D, please!

That will be perfect!

Aha, who doodled a random line on this page! It's so annoying!!!

Nope!

I now need you to get rid of the perfectionism, get rid of OCD (obsessive-compulsive disorder), get rid of the need for flawless in your life. These are big blockers of your productivity and creativity.

I now need you to start to appreciate the adorable pictures and the cute doodle line above – everything stays where they are, no changes – it's also a beauty, isn't it. Do you like them now?

Now, I need you to start living with imperfection; imperfection is the next level of perfection. Just simply enjoy the creative process!

Step Two: Upgrade YOUR thinking!

There's always more than one way to 'skin' a 'sheep'

When you come across difficult situations next time, consider the following:

There's always more than one way to 'skin' a 'sheep'.	There's always option B, option C, option D… option 'infinite'.

If you take your time, everything is figuroutable (figure+out+able).

Why 'there's more than one way to skin a **cat**'?

Why are we skinning a cat, why not a dog ,

a sheep ,

a rabbit

or other animals – though it's all too brutal and illegal in fact.

Replace self-discipline with self-doing

'Self-discipline' is such a hot word on social media these days. Raise your hand if you feel self-discipline is an intimidating word that scares you away. Nod if you feel self-discipline is a quality that only successful people possess.

Let's stop worrying.

Let's upgrade our mindset and upgrade the word 'self-discipline' to 'self-doing', or just 'doing'. Does it sound better, less intimidating and give you a feeling of something achievable?

Here's my secret sauce to keep myself doing every day. I call it 'I can every day':

- ∞ If I breath every day, I can do something creative every day.
- ∞ If I brush my teeth every day, I can eat healthy every day.
- ∞ If I eat every day, I can exercise every day.
- ∞ If I never do drugs, I can also not touch social media.

Let's practise the reverse thinking skill. With an 'I can every day' idea, I now invent an 'I'd not do if I can't' idea, e.g. I'd rather not browse through social media if I know I can't stop after half an hour.

All we're doing here is reinforcing a concept in your mind: self-doing is easily achievable. Do it every day, even like just one minute. It'll become second nature to you in no time, just like brushing your teeth or washing your face effortless.

Now clap your hands if you agree with me, stomp your feet if you disagree, or blink your eyes if you have just generated a new idea on 'self-discipline'.

Step Two: Upgrade YOUR thinking!

Practise your thinking once again

Up to now (if you're reading the book front to back), I imagine you've mastered heaps of creative tools, creative ways of thinking. Let's put it into the practice once again.

What are your brilliant imaginations for the following shapes? Add your answers after each of the shapes. The rule here:

- ∞ The first **rule**: don't refer to the next page until you've done the exercise. The **trick** here: picking other people's brains could limit your thinking initially.

- ∞ The second **rule**: once you've done your activities, flick to the next page, and see if we have come up something similar. And then take another look at these shapes and see if you've come up with other creative ideas on this page. The **trick** here: Once you've done your own thinking, picking other's brain will lead your thinking to another unbelievable level.

Infinite Ways to Stay Creative

My creative thinking is now revealed.

___	Chinese character One	◯	A snowball	▯	My mobile phone	△	A mountain
___	A pool cue	◯	Sun, moon or earth	▯	My home door	△	House roof
___	Peaceful ocean	◯	A plate (someone just ate up a delicious meal!)	▯	My lottery winning ticket	△	The tip of a christmas tree

Now I need you to think them once again. Do something about these brilliant shapes. What would you do?

Step Two: Upgrade YOUR thinking!

I reckon lots of you will colour them or add in something into the graphs. Below are some examples. Make them prettier or uglier – it doesn't matter, it's all art, well done!

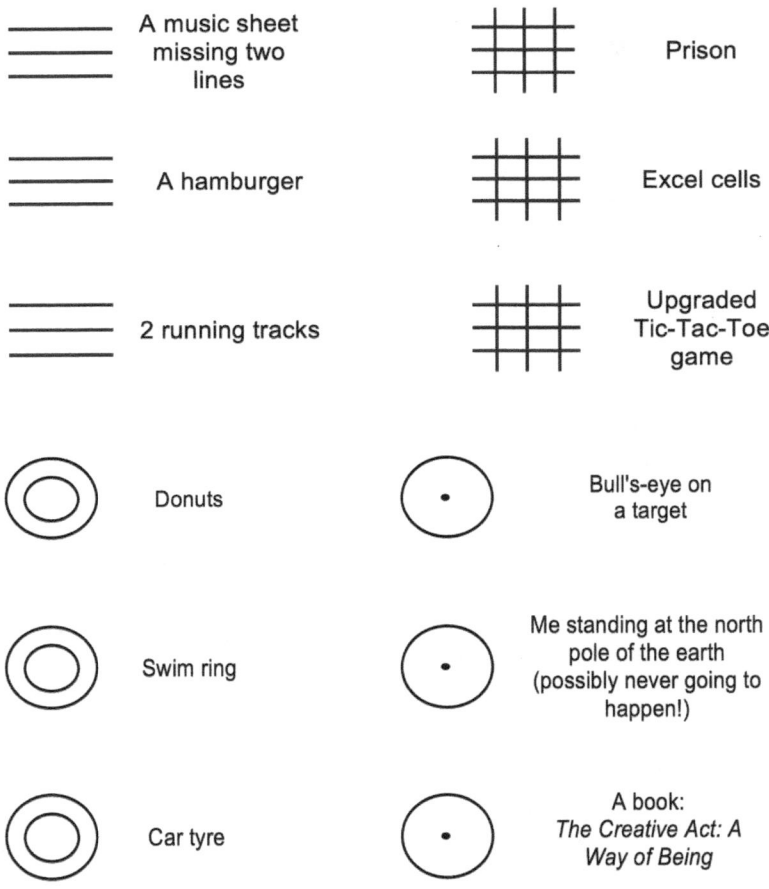

But have you ever thought about removing parts of the shapes, or even make them disappear completely from the paper ('disappear' sounds a bit horror here 😱), instead of adding it? Or even take a longer-term view, and these shapes are moving, not static. What will you get?

Infinite Ways to Stay Creative

Ways to upgrade your thinking – A LOT – INFINITE, in fact!

Infinite ways of thinking? Yes, as long as you're creative enough. One strategy to upgrade your thinking is to:

- ∞ add
- ∞ remove
- ∞ change
- ∞ deny.

Let's put it into practice. Say I'm having a hard time completing my to-do list. Why not turn your diary into a 'not-to-do' list? Or a mixed of 'not-to-do' or 'to-do' lists? If putting down 'spending 1 hour on studying' sounds intimidating, I'd use 'not watching TV' today. I'm an absolute winner if I can get this not-to-do list done.

Another strategy is to invent new concepts based on current knowledge. People often agree: 'less is more'. I'd extend it to 'Yin is Yang', 'slow is fast', 'low is high', 'bad is good', 'lose is win'. Did you see a patten here, and do you agree with me on life wisdom?

The simplest way of thinking is to trust your intuition, your gut feeling, or you can call it a hunch. This is an unconscious thought process and it's our unique way to connect with the universe. When something doesn't feel right, you know it directly, which doesn't need any logical thinking. Hush! Women's intuition is mostly accurate when they sense that their husband is cheating.

By far, I'm sure you've identified your unique way of thinking things now, forward thinking, backward thinking, reverse thinking, flip thinking, critical thinking, abstract thinking, creative thinking, divergent or convergent thinking, you name it.

Once you've discovered your infinite way of thinking, nothing is impossible.

Austin Kleon, in his *Steal Like an Artist* book, says that 99% of art is bribery. I'd say 99.9% of art is bribery. What thinking strategy I'm applying here?

∞ Step One: Start **YOUR** running, right now!

By now, you've gathered your magic tools and your powerful ideas. Congratulations creative ladies and gents! I'm super proud of you.

What to do next?

RUN! Run for it, the fabulous creative artist!

The prefect time to start with your creativity journey is always NOW.

Start working on it, run for it, and leave the legacy to the world that you'd be proud of, and everyone will be proud of!

Run for it, RIGHT NOW

In 2022, I attended Jock Zonfrillo's book launch to celebrate his book *The Last Shot*. Jock was one of the judges on MasterChef Australia. I'm a MasterChef super-fan. I was thrilled with Jock's signature and message to me, 'Jessie, give more than you take.' Wow, these words are still kept in my heart.

A year later, Jock Zonfrillo passed away at the age of 46.

I just simply couldn't believe it. I cried when I was watching MasterChef Australia that year – Jock was no longer with us, with the food he loved and the love he gave to his profession and the world.

RIP.

(Silence...)

People are born every day. People die every day. Death is the fate that no one can avoid.

If you're no longer around tomorrow or if you could take another chance to live again, what are the things you'd like to do or achieve, then do it now, right now. Don't wait another millisecond. Just simply do it now, run for it! Keep this 'do it now, run for it' principle all the time.

You desire to take your creativity off, start it now, run, the fabulous creative artist, run! Use the space below and create something RIGHT NOW. Your time starts NOW!

Step One: Start YOUR running, right now!

 Sparks creativity in your daily routine

No doubt, you have a busy schedule, like everyone does these days. What if I tell you that you can practise your bubbly and sparkling ideas super easily just in your daily routine?

What if I tell you most of my writing or creative ideas are generated while I'm:

- ∞ in the shower or bath (sorry, naked)
- ∞ driving in a car (with Fox radio on)
- ∞ jogging or walking alone (no podcast)
- ∞ sitting on a chair or lying on the bed quietly (with a face mask on)
- ∞ having some alcohol (beer, wine, Chinese sprit, cocktails…all did the work)
- ∞ waking up in the morning (before touching my phone)
- ∞ before bed (after putting down my phone)
- ∞ focusing on the brainless and repetitive tasks at work (to keep my brain in active)
- ∞ reading books (even just flicking through books at the bookstore, any genre)
- ∞ on the toilet (sorry, 'disgusting' here).

What are your ways to operate your idea-generation machine, bits and pieces, here and there, this and that? These creative-skill practices even add spice to your life, hot, sweet, sour, bitter, don't they?

Take super-super-super-quick notes

When an idea sparks or a 'Eureka' moment hits, write it down immediately, immediately, immediately, please, please, please. The idea could disappear in just a milli-milli-milli second.

So I encourage you to keep a habit of 'taking super-super-super-quick notes'. My phone is my magic tool for doing this. Just simply open the Notes app. I'll jot down my ideas there super quickly. It doesn't have to be a perfect complete sentence, just a couple of words or just one word will do the job. It's just a two-second job.

When I need them, too easy, simply go to my Notes app. All my brilliant ideas store there, waving at me.

As you can see, it's effortless, a two-second job, which helps me collect ideas and use them at my leisure. I don't have to search for them again in my brain, which could just disappear forever, no matter how hard I'm searching for later.

Step One: Start YOUR running, right now!

Choose an activity, any except…

When you have 1 hour of free time during the day, which one of the two activities would you prefer on each of the infinite point (∞) below? Use rainbow colours to highlight the activity you desire to do and black colour to cross out the activity that you feel you shouldn't do.

- ∞ **do nothing** vs. looking at YouTube videos
- ∞ **play sports** vs. browsing on Instagram
- ∞ **have a relax spa** vs. checking out Tweets
- ∞ **go for a drive** vs. clicking through Facebook
- ∞ **exercise** vs. flicking through TikTok
- ∞ **draw** vs. chatting on WhatsApp or WeChat Group
- ∞ _____ vs. watching TV dramas.

Following the pattern in the infinite points above, fill in an activity that you'd like to do in your spare time on the wavy line.

Whenever possible, I'd select the first option to do. Sure, I've missed out the new TV dramas or movies that my friends are watching. When they talk about it, I have no clue what they're talking about. So what. Instead I spent my time producing my creative projects. What I've gained is two books so far. To me, this is more meaningful and purposeful.

Let's do some reverse thinking: whoever chooses the second option above also misses out time spent on being creative and getting the fun part of staying creative.

If you find it hard to put down your device, just delete those apps that kill most of your free time. You'll forget them soon enough.

Force yourself to go for the first bold option: just pick up one activity except engaging with digital products. If you still find it hard – keep reading on.

Infinite Ways to Stay Creative

Digital addiction is a new norm?

Tear this page out RIGHT NOW.

What? What the heck?

Yes, you do not hear (read) it wrong. Do it just after reading through this page – tear this page out, cut it off, or just do whatever sparks you on the page **RIGHT NOW**. Just make best use of this piece of paper – do not waste the paper; protect the forest.

Why are we doing the above activity? I'd like to reinforce here again that you should fill in your free time with non-digital activities, any non-digital activities, just like the one we're doing right now.

I'm amazed how easily I'm addicted to digital devices – how comfy just lying down on my bed, holding it in my hand, without doing any active thinking, just watching videos created by others – just for 5 minutes. But then 5 minutes turns into half an hour, then 1 hour, 3 hours, almost the whole day – non–stoppable.

Are we all in the same boat?

I'm hoping you're in a totally different means of transportation with me/us, be it skateboard, bicycle, tuk-tuk, lorry, canoe, bus, car, plane, rocket, _____ be whatever it is.

Let your brain wonder and write down some more means of transportation on the wavy line above.

I can't believe we humans fall in love and become addicted so quickly with these little smart phones or tablets – they are the real drugs but never make you feel they're drugs at all.

Have you torn out the page now? You should have.

Step One: Start YOUR running, right now!

Seriously, you can stop your digital addiction!

Now let's find the most effective medicine for you to cure your digital addition.

The scope here is to remove your digital addiction to useless, meaningless contents that only brings short term pleasure or excitement, and stops you from being creative.

Medicine 1: Use one sentence to persuade yourself to reduce the addiction to your digital devices. Below are three examples, and give your interesting answers on the wavy lines:

- ∞ STOP USING IT!
- ∞ it's harmful to your eyes and health
- ∞ I must be the master not the slave
- ∞ _____

Medicine 2: Applying the 'I can every day' idea in Topic 30 'Replace self-discipline with self-doing' will help: if I can eat every day, I definitely can spend more time on doing something creative every day. Once you start focusing on your creative projects, you'll spend less time on browsing through useless contents on digital products as a time killer.

Medicine 3: Set up rules for yourself, like DO NOT TOUCH MY PHONE when I'm:

- ∞ waking up
- ∞ focusing on work or study
- ∞ riding a train
- ∞ sitting on the toilet
- ∞ going to bed.

And do not break these rules!!!

Medicine 4: Upgrade your mindset. Use what you've learned in Topic 42 'Upgrade your mindset, as a fabulous creative artist'. Calm down, have a think, in the long run, do these videos really bring you anything, any solid results? Probably not.

So it's a fake and superficial pleasure, which isn't a real pleasure. I'd call them 'long term pain', or 'long term meaningless'. Indulging in them day and night will kill almost all your creativity that you're born with. Do you still want this 'long term pain'?

Seriously, put down the phone for at least one hour a day, and start focusing on our creativity brain.

Hush! There's another medicine: technology. Use technology to help you stay off technology. Download the apps that can warn you and lock your phone if you're going over a certain amount of time on your devices. I spotted this good digital-detox strategy while browsing through the social media, so now I 'copy' and 'paste' it into my book. Then should we be completely off social media?

Step One: Start YOUR running, right now!

Put your not-so-good habitsssss into sleep

We all have those so called not-so-good habits, one or two or more. Wait, why don't you call it 'bad habits'. Well, as we've learned in Topic 39 'Words have their power', using positive words brings us energy and a creative mind. So 'not so **good**' is better than '**bad**'.

These not-so-good habits are massive blocks. So let's identify them and quietly put them to sleep. Possible not-so-good habits include:

- ∞ nail biting
- ∞ phone addictive
- ∞ insufficient sleep
- ∞ alcohol abuse
- ∞ non-stop smoking
- ∞ constant complaining
- ∞ habitually lying
- ∞ not exercising
- ∞ staying dehydrated
- ∞ unhealthy eating
- ∞ skipping breakfast
- ∞ excessive profanity
- ∞ spending uncontrollably.

OMG, this list could go on and on.

Did you spot any pattens in the above list? Right, I'm limiting myself to just using two English words here. Do we count 'non-stop smoking' two words or three words?

Now challenge yourself to add more those not-so-good habits with three words in any blank or non-blank area on this page. An example could be eating junk food or spitting in public.

Why not put it down in the sticky notes below, instead of the infinite list format? Which format do you like better?

Step One: Start YOUR running, right now!

Discover your creativity projectsssss

Let's explore creativity projectssssss that you can do in your free time. They have a nickname, called 'hobbiesssss'. Hobbies are not your jobbies (job). They are supposed to bring you purely joy, not koy, loy, moy, noy (Oops, are these even words? They appear here for rhyming purpose).

Engaging in hobbies is such a rewarding activity. It creates a space in our brain that soothes us and calms us down.

So, moving to the exciting part! Let's explore hobbiesssss as much as we can. Add more to the tennis balls below, pick up the ones that you'd like to work on, and then let these tennis balls keep rolling.

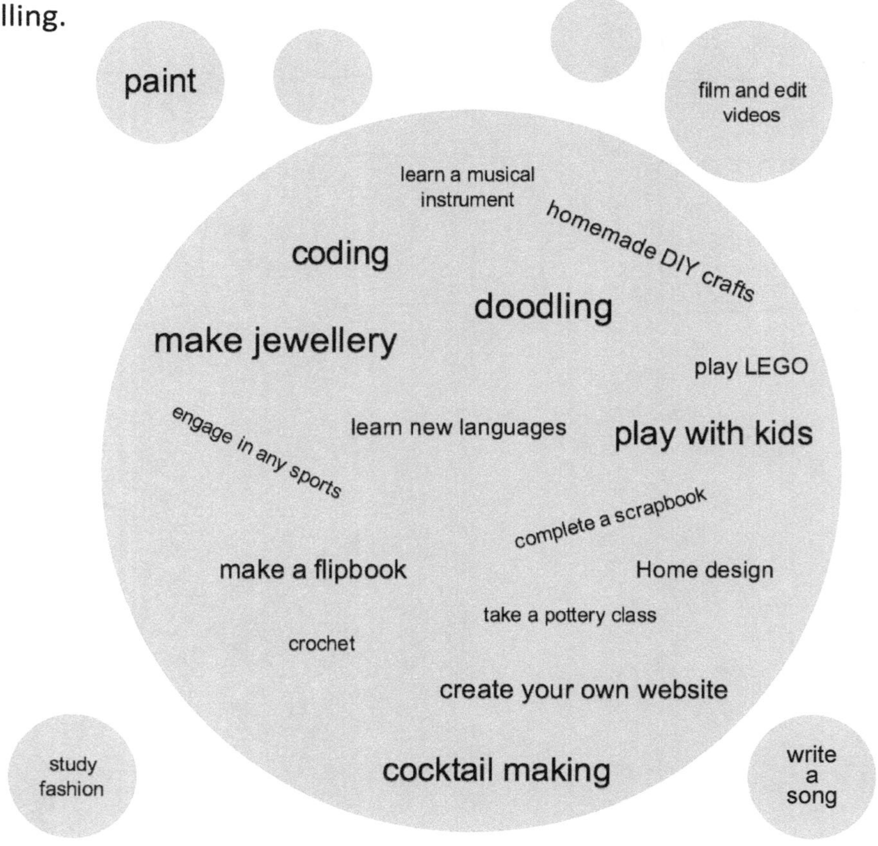

- paint
- film and edit videos
- learn a musical instrument
- homemade DIY crafts
- coding
- doodling
- make jewellery
- play LEGO
- engage in any sports
- learn new languages
- play with kids
- complete a scrapbook
- make a flipbook
- Home design
- take a pottery class
- crochet
- create your own website
- study fashion
- cocktail making
- write a song

Stack your boxes

If you haven't discovered that one activity or few activities that you'd like to do over the time, no worries, let's count your boxes (your stock) first. Each of us has a least one of the boxes, representing our past experiences, things we've tried or been interested in. I'll show you what I have got.

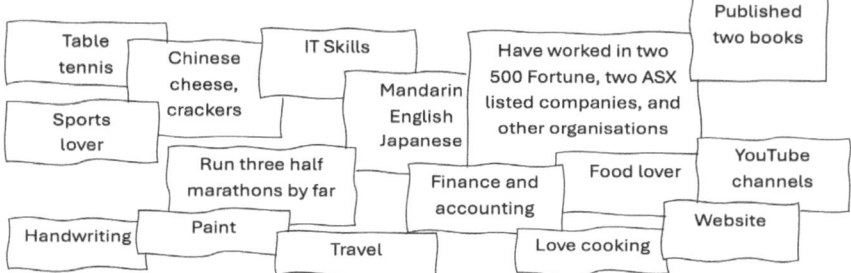

Are these boxes not fancy at all? Well, I love simple stuff. These are part of my boxes. I can keep working and building on it. One day, I can stack them into the Dubai Burj Khalifa Tower, Tokyo Skytree Tower, Lotte World Tower or any tower in my own design.

Some boxes are small while some are big. Some are solid while some might need more work. It doesn't matter how they're intertwined, stacked or maybe they just seem irrelevant with each other right in the moment. All you do is to display all your boxes and keep digging it deeper and keep building more. One day, when you open one of the boxes, the others would be open automatically, potentially.

Now draw your boxes 📦 in the space provided, and see how you'll stack them all over artistically, to build your own tower.

Step One: Start YOUR running, right now!

Have a creative heart of gold

Have a creative heart of gold. Silver or bronze isn't up to the standard. This should be one of your basic principles for creativity. Be gentle to yourself and spread your love, your artwork to the people around you and to the world.

Colour your creative heart in the below. You're **the** most, **fabulous, creative, artist!**

Are you annoyed visually with each of the above hearts being arranged not in a neat order? Jump back to Topic 32 Appreciate the beauty of imperfection and review the page twice again if you are.

Try things

When publishing my first book, I was asked which font I'd like to use as some fonts are good for reading on paper, and some are easier on eyes if you choose to read online.

Out of curiosity, I'm just trying out how different fonts look like on paper. Can you tell the difference in them, which are chosen from Microsoft Word software.

ART ART **ART** ᴀʀᴛ 𝒜𝑅𝒯 ART **ART** ART ART ART ART ART ART 𝒜𝑅𝒯 ART **ART ART ART**

ART ART ART ART 𝒜𝑅𝒯 *ART* ART ART ART **ART** **A R T** 𝒜𝑅𝒯 ART 𝒶𝓇𝓉 **ART**

𝒜𝑅𝒯 ART ✂❄❋ ➛☑☒ ↩☞︎⌃ 🏰 ✆▢◆ ⌘➈❶ ⇨△◀ ✓✗📄

Question: how many examples of 'art' did you count? I bet you're now going back to check it out. Give me a high five here if I'm right! 🙌

Wait, what are the last eight with the cute icons? They're 'ART' and 'art' in Wingdings, Wingdings 2, Wingdings 3, Webdings, respectively.

Wow, I'm getting super-excited now – to see so many fascinating fonts. Talking about the beautiful typograph available on computers, Steve Jobs came into my mind, who included it in the Mac. Should we say thank you to the one of the greatest innovators in the world?

What I'm illustrating here is that when you try things, even little things, it can bring you the excitement, knowledge, experience that further grows your creativity, and it might transform your life one day – you never know!

Step One: Start YOUR running, right now!

So let's not waste any time. List things you'd like to try in the below and start to experiment them one by one. I'm super excited for you!

Read AMAP

What does AMAP in the title stand for? Bingo! I just created a new buzz word, an abbreviated version of 'as many as possible'.

Why should we read, and read AMAP? I'd encourage you to re-read AMAP.

Every book is the result of an author's thoughts and their development day after day, so reading no doubt helps produce more brilliant creative work for you.

Building a Second Brain by Tiago Forte is an eye-opening book which gives us methods to activate our second-brain superpowers for creative potential in this digital world. Why can't we build up the third, the fourth? Do we even have the third and the fourth brain?

While I was enjoying reading the book *Let the Elephants Run – Unlock Your Creativity and Change Everything* by David Usher, I would question why it's called 'Let the elephants run'? Why the author didn't call it:

- ∞ Let the penguin roar
- ∞ Let the pigs fly
- ∞ Let the mosquito not sting you
- ∞ Let the fish sleep (Do fish even sleep? How do you know if they do?)
- ∞ Prevent the dog from barking
- ∞ Stop being stung by mozzie
- ∞ Force the Myna birds to not eat apples on your apple tree
- ∞ Let myself be creative.

Step One: Start YOUR running, right now!

The Artist's Way by Julia Cameron is the book that lots of my creator friends have recommended. The key takeaway, for me, is to just to write three pages first thing in the morning, write anything, whatever you'd like to do on the page. I'd upgrade Julia's idea – we don't have to do three pages in the morning, one page is good enough, or even just put down one or two sentences in the Notes of your phone is super-duper, whatever thoughts flow through at that moment in the morning.

See, I'm stealing and questioning these ideas by reading, from other authors, combining theirs, summarising theirs, upgrading theirs, and they become mine, and now yours.

Visit art, exhibitions and museums

I'm lucky that I live in Melbourne, a vibrant city with art everywhere. Visiting art galleries, exhibitions and museums over the years ignites my creativity and inspires me in many big ways. I'd encourage you to do so in your free time.

I'll take you through three parts of exhibitions that I've been to:

1. **Triennial** by National Gallery of Victoria: A real banana was taped to the gallery wall. The banana is supposed to be replaced every seven to ten days. Use your imagination to tape the banana below onto the wall.

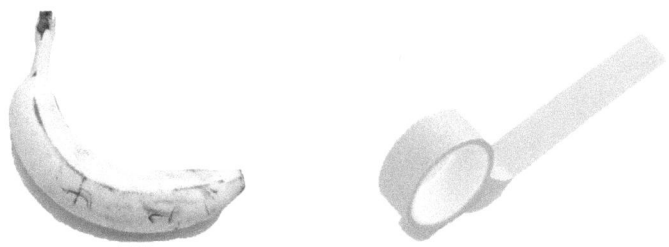

2. Use the basic shapes (below) from **Peter Tyndall**'s art, tell me what you can see. Peter Tyndall saw lots of things and made them all into artwork.

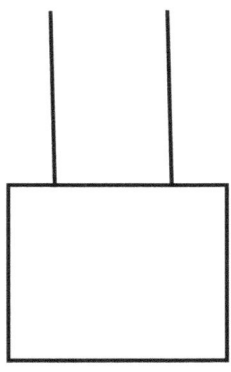

Step One: Start YOUR running, right now!

3. **'Girl with Balloon' artwork** is one of the **Banksy**'s most famous pieces, which was shredded just after the artwork was sold for more than one million dollars at auction. Banksy says, 'A lot of people never use their initiative because no-one told them to'. He also says 'Sometimes I feel so sick at the state of the world I can't even finish my second apple 🍎 pie 🥧 '. I learned this when visiting **The Art of Banksy: 'Without Limits'**.

Shout out your bloody hard work

As soon as you've started on your creative work, start to show it off. Show it off to your family, your friends, your community buddies, or even people you don't know, online, offline, in the country, out of the country. If the chocolate bar below represents the progress of your creative work, mark your current position. See how much bloody hard work you've done.

-10%   0%   100%   150%

Then make sure you share your working-in-progress artwork with the whole world, shout out **loud, loud and aloud!**

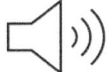

Then continue to shout out **loud, loud and aloud!**

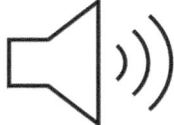

Then continue to shout out **loud, loud and aloud!**

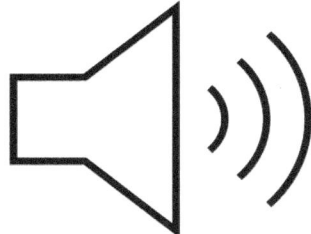

Step One: Start YOUR running, right now!

Set up a 30-day challenge

Why not set up a 30-day challenge? Just simply put down an easy and healthy 'task' for each day and get the challenge completed one by one in the next following 30 days. Below is an example and help me complete the icons that are missing.

30-day challenge

Day 1 Sleep early	Day 2 Make a smile	Day 3 Visit a bookstore	Day 4 Watch the sunset	Day 5 Movie night
Day 6 Learn a new song	Day 7 Cook a meal	Day 8 Clean my closet	Day 9 Doodle	Day 10 Call my best friend
Day 11 Eat a rainbow	Day 12 Stretch	Day 13 Do a mask	Day 14 DIY a thing	Day 15 Spend no money
Day 16 Say hello to a stranger	Day 17 Buy fresh flowers	Day 18 Kiss my family	Day 19 Ignite the candle	Day 20 Take a warm bath
Day 21 Go for a walk	Day 22 Try a new restaurant	Day 23 Screen free day	Day 24 Take a photo	Day 25 Go shopping
Day 26 Let the sunshine in	Day 27 Write one page journal	Day 28 Plan next trip	Day 29 Sleep in	Day 30 Celebrate

Play, rest and sleep

Attention please, attention please: 'All work and no play makes Jack a dull boy, Jenny a dull girl.' The first part of the quote was collected in James Howell's *Proverbs* in 1659. Second part? I added it in.

Some say, 'All play and no work makes Jack a mere toy.' It seems that we need to find a balance between work and play. Play, rest and sleep in turn nurtures your fabulous creativity ability and your brilliant artwork. Keep below in mind all the time:

No play, no creativity.

No rest, no creativity.

No sleep, no creativity.

Now add two more elements contributing to a better artwork in the blank gift box below.

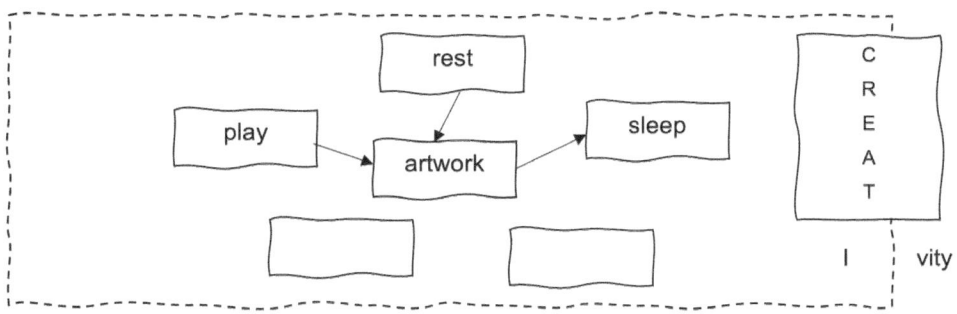

Wait, did you spot an 'error' ('errors') in the graph above.

Well – done!

Now, put down the book and go take a break – play, rest, sleep, whatever makes you excited now.

Step One: Start YOUR running, right now!

Celebrate early mornings, or dark nights

Let's practise your creativity. Write down a few words in the wavy rectangular below, guess what the author is trying to say.

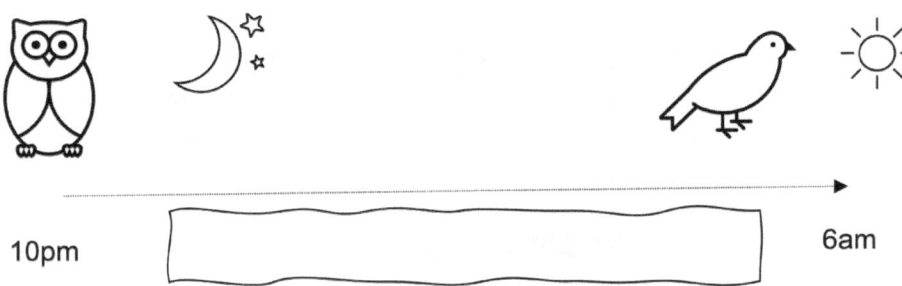

Books are out there talking about the miracle morning, encourage people to join the 5am club, and even give tips for super lazy people on how to wake early. Apple CEO Tim Cook starts his morning before 4am. Xerox CEO Ursula Burns rises before 5.30am. Virgin Group founder and chairman Richard Branson gets up before 6am… Lots of successful people would use their early morning for exercise, reading, research, work, etc.

I'm also an early riser, waking up before 6am. I'd say the early birds get better worms. My creativity and productivity are the best during that time. It's me time – when I have a clear and super creative mind without any disturbances.

Your creativity is also better in the dim light of late night.

So no matter if you're a night owl or an early bird, let's not waste the best time of the day. Let's use it well and celebrate it!

What does a night owl get?

10
Do it consistently until...

Creativity is born with, but you need to keep using it and crafting it. It's a skill that can be un-un-learned, unlearned, relearned, re-re-learned. It's like our muscles, which you can't build in one day. Who do you think mostly possible to get their six-pack abs in one year's time, Alex or Arthur?

- ∞ **Alex:** goes to gym and works out for only ten minutes every day.
- ∞ **Arthur:** goes to gym and works out for half a day but only three times a month.

I bet Alex will win the competition and be more fit in the end.

To build up your creativity muscles, you don't have to show up every single day, like what Alex does. 80%, 90% of showing up rate is great, which is enough to keep your creative momentum going. Only small pieces each time will do the magic work.

The golden key 🗝 is consistency.

Do, repeat, do, repeat, do, repeat, until you, the creative monster, make your creative habit into a routine, just as easy as brushing your teeth every day. But this is way much more fun than brushing your teeth! Once it becomes your habit, it's like a drug addiction. You can't get rid of it in your system anymore.

Then keep working on it until **the magic happens** 🪄.

Step One: Start YOUR running, right now!

9 Suck and stuck?

aaaaaaaaaaaaaaaaaaaaaaaaaaaaaaaaaaaaaaaaaaaaaaaaaa!!!

What are we doing here?

When you're stuck in your projects, the feeling sucks, you're going nowhere, you run out all your ideas, it's your block. I get you completely. We all have such moments.

What would I normally do?

I literally just scream out (at home)! Or just yell out multiple Chinese '啊(a)' (shown above) to release my inner voice, expressing my struggles.

Of course, this only helps with my emotional parts. Reality? For the book I'm working on, I'd still turn on my laptop, open up the working file, even just typing one word, I'd do it because I'm moving forward. It's that simple! I'd then surprisingly find that one word somehow becomes a sentence, then a paragraph. Sometimes, even on bad days, I could produce some surprisingly good content.

From the creator's high to the creator's low, it's a path that we'll come across along the journey. I start liking this part of the journey – as once you've broken through, your low later becomes your new high in the end – one of the best parts!

What if I just can't think of any things for my projects, it's been couple of days, I'm so sick of it. No big deal. I'd take it easy and take breaks (not forever breaks though). I'd put it out of my sight, out of my mind. I'd indulge myself for a while:

- ∞ lying in bed, sofa, bean bag, flicking through my phone

- ∞ spending time with family and friends
- ∞ walking in nature
- ∞ engaging in other creative projects.

Just do anything except this bloody project that is causing a headache right now! Let it sleep. Don't wake it up. Give it days or months if you don't have a deadline. When you're back with a fresh mind, increased knowledge and new experiences, you'll bring your project to a level that you never thought you'd reach.

Step One: Start YOUR running, right now!

Have the patience of a saint

Well done! You've taken off running consistently for your creative goal, a fabulous creative artist, remember Topic 44!

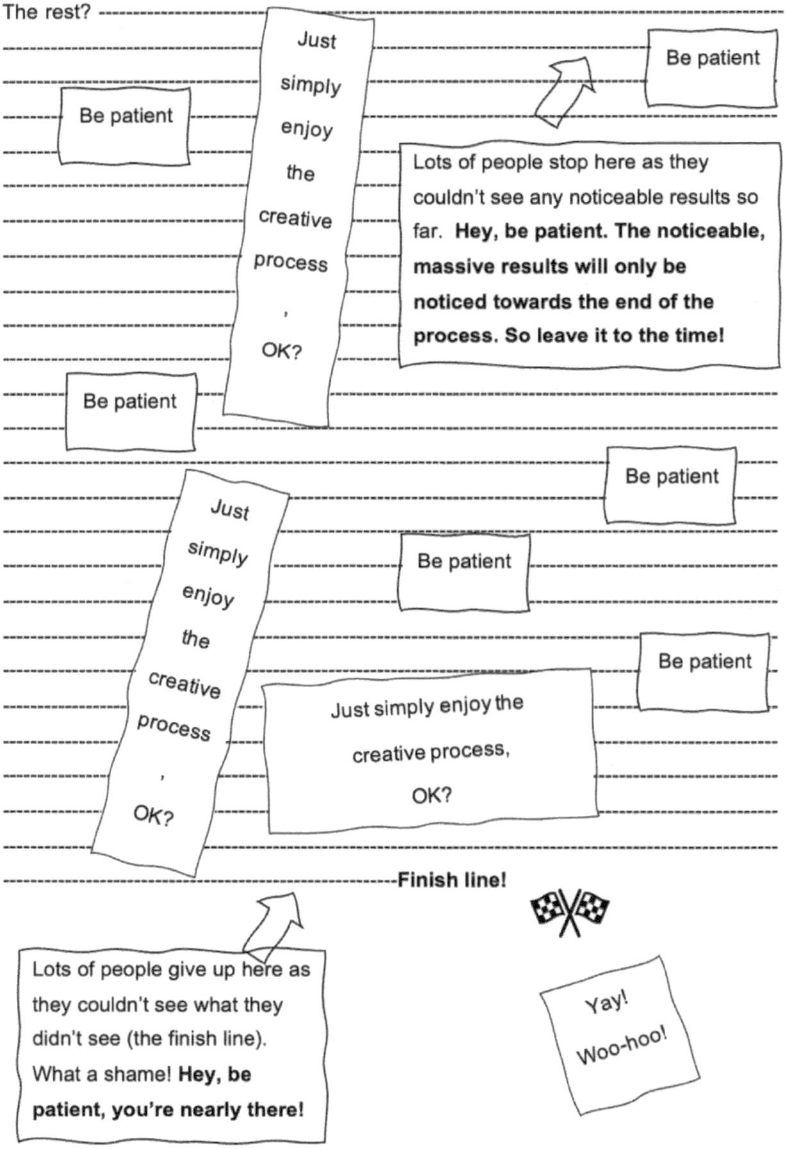

The rest?

Be patient

Just simply enjoy the creative process, OK?

Be patient

Lots of people stop here as they couldn't see any noticeable results so far. **Hey, be patient. The noticeable, massive results will only be noticed towards the end of the process. So leave it to the time!**

Be patient

Be patient

Just simply enjoy the creative process, OK?

Be patient

Just simply enjoy the creative process, OK?

Be patient

----Finish line!

Lots of people give up here as they couldn't see what they didn't see (the finish line). What a shame! **Hey, be patient, you're nearly there!**

Yay! Woo-hoo!

Deliver on your commitment

Dear fabulous creative artists, are you still in the game, the game to practise your creativity skills every day and keep working on your creative projects?

How much effort have you been putting in? Make a mark on the line down below. Zero represents nil effort, and 100 represents 'you're going all in'.

0 ———————————————————— 100

Where did you put your mark?

I hope you didn't put less or equal to 100%. Why? I hope you thought outside the box, are willing to extend that line, and put down a mark outside of the line, say 200%, or do whatever it takes to achieve your creative dreams.

What are your creative dreams? Have you figured them out? To become a world-class TV creator? To be a popular music star? To work with Elon Musk on some amazing projects? To be more creative at your current job? To be creative for a family get-together? To publish a book?

Let us know your creative dreams down here:

Remember as you go, make your creative projects loud and aloud, and share them with the world!

Step One: Start YOUR running, right now!

Dreams without actions are only daydreaming. Wake up, the fabulous creative artist, take your actions RIGHT NOW, run for it, deliver your commitments, and become that fabulous creative artist you've been dreaming of.

Nothing is impossible with a willing heart and raw determination. You'll get there, eventually.

Ways to do – A LOT – INFINITE!

The purpose of the book really is to help you explore and build up your ways to improve your creative quotient (CQ), consistently.

I'm hoping you're not just dreaming about your creativity; I'm hoping you do not let your New Year's resolution become your Next Year's resolution again, again and again.

Apart from what we've gone through so far in the book, I'll put down some extra brilliant ways to bring your creativity to the next level. Think hard and put down your brilliant ways to **achieve** your creativity dream, in wherever you'd like.

- ∞ stay healthy
- ∞ meditate daily
- ∞ appreciate things
- ∞ keep going
- ∞ remove self-doubt
- ∞ focus on yourself
- ∞ build up good habits
- ∞ learn to say 'no'
- ∞ learn like a polymath
- ∞ go travelling
- ∞ embrace the world
- ∞ keep my place clean
- ∞ being in the right relationship
- ∞ never fear things go wrong
- ∞ others' opinions are irrelevant to me
- ∞ _____
- ∞ _____
- ∞ _____
- ∞ _____

Keep this in mind: you're in charge of your own CQ and you're responsible for it. So take your bloody action to run for it, to keep nurturing it.

∞ Step Zero: From Zero to Aero

In this chapter, let's go back to 'square zero' together. This doesn't mean we're going backwards on the creative journey. Instead, we should keep looking at the start point and keep reminding ourselves – why did we start Step One, Two, Three... initially.

From Zero to Aero, zero in the dictionary is defined as a number, meaning no quantity or nothing. Aero is an adjective, meaning of 'air' or 'atmosphere'.

From the zero to aero, we would come across yero, xero, wero, vero, uero, tero, sero, rero, qero, pero, oero, nero, mero, lero, kero, jero, iero, hero, gero, fero, eero, dero, cero, bero, or even end up with aaero, abero – the possibilities are endless.

So why do we keep looking for ways to improve our creativity, for the joy, for the calm, for the sense of achievement, for the money, for whatever the reasons. Apply what you've learned by reading the book you're holding right now, you're heading to somewhere. Where?

5

About Zero – a page from my first book

From Zero, yeah, we start zero in our creativity journey. The start point doesn't have to be perfect (review Topic 32 of 'Appreciate the beauty of imperfection' twice again if you haven't made it into your mindset). Give a laugh on what I put down initially on one page in my first book: *The English Builder!*

DAY 102 创意点子 (BE CREATIVE)

Nothing is unachievable with your sparking ideas. Liberate your creativity.
Harness your creativity.
Sharpen your creativity.
Unlock your creativity.
Stimulate your creativity.

IDEAS:
Big ideas
Bright ideas
Creative ideas
Newborn ideas = New ideas
Birth new ideas
Original ideas
Crisp ideas
Inflated ideas
Madcap idea = crazy and unlikely to succeed
Nutty ideas = crazy [informal.]
Wacky ideas [古怪的 奇怪的]
- ∞ Spiced-up ideas [interesting, lively or sexy]
- ∞ Half-baked ideas 想法不成熟的
- ∞ Rotten ideas 搜主意

A stillborn idea [从一开始就夭折的] => Still, it's an idea!

THINKING:
Lateral thinking

Forward-thinking
Blue-sky thinking
Black-and-white thinking [all-or-nothing thinking=splitting]
Think outside the box.
Think outside the square.
Think on your feet.
Think the unthinkable.
Think beyond convection.

AN AHA MOMENT:

An eureka moment

Aha, a light bulb moment!

Creativity is a learned skill. To become innovative,

- Draw circles in one minute as many as you can.

- Get yourself bored. A boring time helps you generate most ideas.

- Note down your ideas immediately whenever it comes up. If you don't, they may disappear instantly.

- There are so many other ways to develop a natural default way of creative thinking. Use your imagination. Inspiration starts here.

4

About Aero – the same page from my first book

Well, well, well. As I shared the zero start of my very first draft of my first manuscript on the previous page, how did you feel about it? The worst book of the century, of the whole human being's history, if this got published? Laugh if out , please, if you like.

Now, let's read through what 'Aero' looks like in the end.

DAY 113

Let's resolve a nine-dot puzzle. You need to connect all the dots with four straight lines without lifting the pen from the paper.

•　　•　　•

•　　•　　•

•　　•　　•

Eureka! The only way to do it is to think outside the box beach [≈ think outside the ~~square~~ squirrel.] Extend your lines outside of the 'box' in the picture above, you'll have the puzzle resolved.

< The term 'eureka' is attributed to the ancient Greek scholar Archimedes. He stepped into a bathtub, noticed that the water level rose. The more he immersed himself in, the more water overflowed. He suddenly realised that the volume of water displaced depended on the volume of the part of his body he was immersed [≈ submerged]. He jumped out of the tub, running naked in street, and shouted 'Eureka! Eureka! Eureka!' (Biello, 2006) This was the moment that he discovered the principle of buoyancy. So a 'eureka' moment is like a light bulb moment [≈ an 'aha!' moment] for sudden inspiration. It means 'I have found it' in Greek. >

< The Eureka Tower is one of the Melbourne's most iconic buildings. The Tower is 297.3m in height. It's named after a rebellion in 1854 Victoria gold rush, called 'Eureka Stockade'. >

Step Zero: From Zero to Aero

Hey, are < > really angled brackets? Could it be they are less-than and greater-than signs? Or is it a broken diamond shape? What do you see? Unleash your creativity. [≈ Harness your creativity. ≈ Sharpen your creativity. ≈ Unlock your creativity. ≈ Stimulate your creativity.]

You may wonder: where is the today's title and drawing behind it? It's not an editing error. Use your imagination to add one.

- If you can't think the unthinkable [≈ can't think beyond conventions], use the below strategies to help generate ideas:
- Draw as many wave lines, circles or squares as you can in 1 minute.
- Get yourself bored on purpose. Take a seat. Don't pick up your phone or turn on the TV or read a book (including the book you're reading right now).
- Take a long shower or a long bath.

What types of ideas did you end up having in each of these situations?

sparking ideas, big ideas, bright ideas, fresh ideas, creative ideas, newborn ideas [≈ new ideas ≈ birth new ideas], original ideas, crisp ideas, inflated ideas, madcap ideas [≈ nutty ideas ≈ crazy ideas], wacky ideas, spiced-up ideas [≈ interesting ideas], half-baked ideas, rotten ideas, unconventional ideas, stillborn ideas

After my first book was published, the above 'Aero' moved to a new 'Zero'. Amazingly, it keeps spiralling up to the infinite possibilities. This will be a similar path with your practice on your creativity nature.

Infinite Ways to Stay Creative

About this book

Drawing a conclusion at each milestone of your projects makes you a better fabulous creative artist each time, moving towards next level of the creativity.

Let's use this book as an example. What is your conclusion about this book? Think about the book from as many perspectives as you can, go wild please.

Here comes my summary on the book. Help me complete the blank lines.

∞ The book's title is '_____'.

∞ The book contains:

- ∞ _____ pages
- ∞ _____ words
- ∞ _____ chapters
- ∞ _____ colours
- ∞ _____ rules
- ∞ _____ pictures
- ∞ _____ words of 'creativity'.

∞ The book has or has not:
- ∞ successfully incorporated all phone emojis
- ∞ failed to inspire me on an interesting topic: creating something real (or unreal).
- ∞ encouraged me/him/her/us/them to create something new (or non-existing).
- ∞ offered me the infinite tools and ways for creation journey on my own
- ∞ be like any other books like no other.

Step Zero: From Zero to Aero

Hey, did you notice that the full stops in the above infinite bullet point are not consistent. From editor's point of view, they should be consistent. From artist's point of view, appreciate the beauty of the imperfection, please!

So let's leave the imperfection just like that. You're not allowed to add or remove the punctuation above.

About the book title

Here are the results of my brainpower when I was thinking about the book titles that didn't make it.

Simple title	Creativity
Boring title	Creativity rules?
Weird title	36.5 things that writing my first book has taught me about creativity
Super short title	(Nothing)
Super long title	Where is the book title? What is the book about? Who is the book for? When was the book published? Why should I read this book? How_____?
Exciting title	What the hell is that ~!@#$%^&*()_+

Look at the 'super-short title', which says 'Nothing'. 'Can you publish a book without a book title?' Google says 'NO'. It seems that this is the rule that I must follow in order to deliver the book to your hand.

For the super long title, is it long enough? What's the title length requirement for a book publishing?

Even on this title there are many other ways to present Infinite Ways to Stay Creative, (e.g. make words upside down, have angles, different colors, and make texts invisible and only when you drop lemon juice on top of it, it'll become visible, on and on).

Ok, let's get back to the business. What on earth is the best title of this book, in your opinion? Help me make the best book title of the year, and ever down below:

Step Zero: From Zero to Aero

About the ∞

Last of all — last (Does this expression even exist in the English world), let's talk about this ∞ symbol from the book title and throughout the book.

What's your interpretation of this symbol?

Below are mine:

- ∞ Double O or Double Zero (why are there double O or double 0 ways to stay creative?)
- ∞ 8 ways (Did the author put it upside down?)
- ∞ U+A74F (what the h*ll is this?)
- ∞ Two eyes (to observe?)
- ∞ It has no meaning, but just an icon that the author uses to illustrate that there are unlimited ways to stay creative in our everyday life, also to keep reminding the reader there are indeed ∞ ways to stay creative.

Can you draw a different symbol that also represents 'Infinite'? 'Infinite' is bigger than what you think. How big is it?

About your creativity

Congratulations, fabulous creative artist! We've just artfully finished reading this book together. Tell me, what is your relationship with your sense of creativity now? Colour, tick, cross what you honestly think.

- ☐ I still couldn't bother!
- ☐ He/she (or It) is still a stranger.
- ☐ We used to be close friends, but not anymore.
- ☐ We're still nurturing each other.
- ☐ Our relationship has ever grown stronger and stronger.
- ☐ None of above.
- ☐ Other.* (State your creative answer down below)

No matter what your creative style is (random, brainstorming has always come to the first step, do as I go, mix of these, none of these), you're well set.

Well done!

Break legs! (Why it's not break arms or fingers?)

INTRODUCTION

You might wonder: Jessie, you're not one of the New York Times' best-selling authors, you're not a celebrity or a popular, motivational speaker on YouTube or TikTok, you have never attended a lesson on how to be creative, and you've never been heard. How dare you share with me how to stay creative?

Well, I **dare to dream**. You should too.

I was happy to 'show off' my lifestyle in my early 20s, or basically it was the lifestyle that I chose to have without awareness, before I started writing my first book or before I had a dream. Let's dive into it straight away.

- [x] I barely woke up and got up in the early morning. If my work started at 9am, I would get up at 8.30am, rushed to the office and had a rushed brekkie at my desk to start a day.

- [x] I could stay up to 2am or 3am in the morning just to binge watch TV series on Netflix during weekdays and weekends too.

- [x] I couldn't stop playing electronic games, one game after another. I wouldn't stop all day until I reached to the next level. By then, I probably would continue with the 'next level' to reach to the level after 'next level', with my unstoppable 'game on' face and ironman 'must be the champion' determination.

- [x] I didn't exercise very often. I enrolled in gym classes but ended up going there for a week or two. Then I would keep 'forgetting' to go there for the rest of the year.

- [x] I didn't know what I was doing every day. Home–Work–Home–Work–Home, day after day, month after month, year after year. Time just flew by like this.

- [x] I didn't quite like making changes. I didn't quite like trying new things or having new experiences unless I was forced to.

- Last but not the least, the list for my lazy lifestyle just goes on and on.

Looking back now, I appreciate those years, the laziness – I would say. It made me understand how these bad habits could break you, making you live aimlessly. In turn, an aimless life creates bad habits, and potentially destroys you in lifelong terms – see every experience counts! (This is one way to upgrade your mindset by seeing things from multiple perspectives. Jump to Topic 42 'Upgrade your mindset, as a fabulous creative artist' if you haven't started the book.)

Well, what changed me? The dream – The moment when I started dreaming of writing and publishing a book.

Starting with typing something down on the screen every day (even though sometimes it's all nonsense words, phrases, or sentences, I started to get up early without any effort, sometimes even as early as 5am or 4am, and still be full of energy for the whole day – this is probably the power of dreams. Wow!

So, if I **dare to dream. You should too.**

And I believe you can actualise your dream. Otherwise, you won't even search 'how to be creative' or won't even buy this book and have that burning desire to read it in the first place.

Up until now, are you still worrying and making wrong assumptions that you have no creativity skills at all? Has this book changed your view about 'creativity'? How would you define the word 'creativity' now? What does the 'creativity' look like to you?

To me, creativity is like an everyday adventure that could lead me anywhere, somewhere or even nowhere! I just simply enjoy this fantastic journey Every. Single. Day now 😅.

Let's change the word of 'creativity' appearing in the book and reduce it into minimum or zero at every place that 'creativity' has

INTRODUCTION

shown up. Everybody gives a try – Two minds are better than one! Two heads, I mean zillions of trillions of heads, everyone's minds. Now interpret the idiom 'Two heads are better than one' in a fun way, and potentially do more for all other funny and interesting idioms or slangs. Examples include 'too many cooks spoil the broth', 'a cup of tea', 'a piece of cake', 'let the ~~cat~~ dog out of the bag'... (We're heading somewhere else now).

In the end/beginning, did you **break the rule** that I set up at the very beginning of the book (the Appendix section)? The rule that said not to come to this Introduction section before starting the book.

If you did, congratulations! You've just practised your very first skill of being creative: breaking the useless, non-sense rules in life! Have a reflection here that in your daily life, which rules are useless and non-sense that you possibly can break?

For those who have followed through the order of the book, go find which rules in the book you should break and which ones you shouldn't. Let's list 26 rules from letter A to letter Z, each. Work on your rules down below and check out my random rules on the next page. If you come up with same rules as mine (what a chance!), high-five then change one!

YOUR FUN RULES:

A	G
B	H
C	I
D	J
E	K
F	L

M	T
N	U
O	V
P	W
Q	X
R	Y
S	Z

MY MAKING-SENSE or NOT-MAKING-SENSE RULES:

Arrive 1 hour earlier for a party	No swearing for the whole month
Break a rule every week	Object others' request
Cook a fine dining meal every weekend	Plant a tree in Royal Botanic Gardens
Draw circles when getting angry	Quit the job immediately if your boss is an asshole
Eat the rainbow for the whole year	Run backwards or weird like Phoebe
Flush toilet every time after use	Slur the noodles
Get a sickie every 1.2 months	Turn off the lights every time when the room is no longer in use
Hide somewhere when parents are coming back home for fun	Use punctuation in a wrong way in book writing and get the readers to spot and correct it
Invent some little things once a week	Volunteer with a charity

INTRODUCTION

Jump the queue to the front (find a proper excuse, please)	Wash hands before eating
Kiss in the train (not to strangers)	X: too hard (I break the rule here!)
Lift up my hand at least once every day	Yell out when being alone
Make a new friend with a street stranger	Zip my fly all the time

I hope you didn't generate all 26 rules (ideas) in one go, or in one day. If you have already, you're absolutely a legend. If not, you're also absolutely a legend!

I didn't create them all in one day. It took me over a year to complete, on and off. Sometimes, the rules were boring, so I scratched them, or sometimes, I didn't have any ideas! For some days, I ran out of ideas completely! I doubted if my work was good enough, good enough to be seen by the public? Let me tell you: artwork is never good enough, so I stopped worrying. (Question: Does perfect artwork exist?)

Keep going, you'll eventually get there.

This is just the creation process. Let's give 'creation process' a fancier name. What do you have in your pocket? Put it down here

---

Here's mine: creation pathways, from zillions of ideas to end product, zero to infinity.

Are your 26 rules (creations) better than mine, than hers, than everyone else? Nope, Are they worse? Nope either. There is no good or bad artwork at all, they're your brilliant thoughts processed at the time being, and they're all brilliant! The key thing here is: All ideas, thoughts and artworks are the results of all wisdoms from us, human beings, fabulous creative artists.

Now go back to your rules, cross out rules that are not allowed to be broken. And tick the rules that you want to break. Add more rules, as why did the English alphabet only have 26 letters? I heard Ampersand (&) was used over 1,500 years ago, as the 27th letter of the English Alphabet. Maybe you can create a new letter or word and make it popular! Genius, another creation process!

Alright, let's get back to the rule. You know how to break the rule, right? Use your hands, arms, legs, feet, or mind, or (Put down your way of breaking here _____). I just need you to break them wisely and artfully.

Phew! If you've followed all my instructions and methodologies throughout the book, congratulations! Breaking the rules is the last piece of the puzzle that I want to share with you.

Now GO BACK to the beginning of the book:

- ∞ If you've broken the first rule of the book, read it from the start.
- ∞ If you haven't broken the rule, review the book once again (Hush, they say, creativity is also a repetition).
- ∞ or why should I start from the *first* chapter?

Up to this point, you've mastered the essence of how to be creative, plus your own amazing personal experiences and your wide range of knowledge. I'm sure you've turned yourself into a creativity pro, the creative monster!

If you disagree with any of opinions that I've made in the book, just go back and cross them out, or even just tear that page out,

INTRODUCTION

and fold it into a paper boat, pants, flowers, bookmarks, origami lantern, one thousand cranes, then stick your pretty artwork in the below blank area.

Or do whatever you like – it's your creative activity now. If you're holding the digital book, oops, you don't have this option but you can do it in your mind.

Now, it's review and reflection time.

Hey, are you aware that review and reflection is also part of creation process – a crucial one – to further boost your creativity!

Let's all head onto Amazon website now.

Search 'Infinite ways to stay creative'. Find this book, go to book review section. Leave a comment, or two, be it your review on the book, your brilliant ideas or whatever you think could trigger and inspire creativity in others. All things are welcomed! 🤗 Just simply **GO WILD**! (though I'm not expecting coarse and offensive language)

Nothing should be holding you back from sharing them with the world.

I'm now curious what we would be ending up having over the years. (Keep a curious and open mind – all the time – something you should keep along your creation journey)

Worst case scenario? No comments, no reviews. You might have saved yourself valuable time on creative projects of your own by not even needing read the book. Well done too! But remember, giving a review or writing down a comment itself is also a creation process – simply practise the skills whenever you can.

Best case scenario? The world is becoming more interesting and innovative because of you, because of your contributions. Be mindful though, I might 'steal' your ideas one day because they're sparkling and inspiring. Others might 'steal' yours too. Be generous with them and share your love with the word, and we should all do the same.

Please describe your relationship with creativity now and state your reason in the box below. Your honest opinions are highly valued.

(word limit:200 characters)

Thank you for your participation.

Here are your chances **to break the bloody rule**: did you provide comments outside the box, break the word limit rules, or didn't put anything down because you've answered a similar questionnaire in Topic 0 'About your creativity'.

Now, let's take a pause here.

I've just had such a wonderful journey with you, my dear readers, on our creativity adventure. I spotted: sun, sea, moon, forest, country road, tigers, kangaroos, penguins, sea gulls, people jogging. I heard: dog barking, keyboard dancing, wind blowing, chin chin cheers, New Year's Eve countdown in the crowd. I felt:

INTRODUCTION

warm, happy, enjoyable, love, joy, pride… What did you see, hear, and feel?

Congratulations! Now we've arrived at a wonderful island more than full of creativity and art. (Oops, are there any grammar mistakes in this sentence? I reckon it doesn't have. It's only how you perceive the grammar mistakes and your definition on what the correct grammar is, isn't it?)

The End (which is also a new beginning)

Infinite Ways to Stay Creative

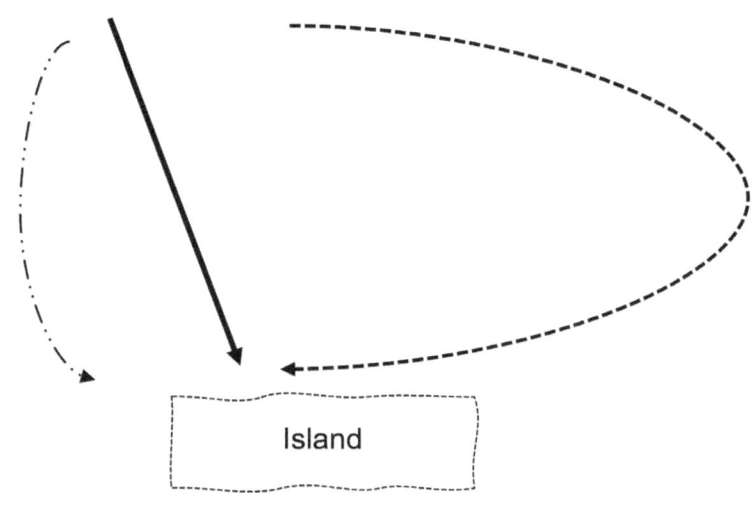

Every end is a new beginning, isn't it?

End isn't a new beginning, is it?

Should we stop here or keep going? You let me know.

Cheers to our creative human nature!

Your creative buddy,

Jessie

TABLE OF CONTENTS

You may wonder: Where is the Table of Contents?

Well, this isn't an editing or printing error. It's a great opportunity for you to review what you've learnt throughout the book.

Based on your memory, create the Table of Contents on the previous page right now. No flicking back the book is allowed in this round.

Once you've done above exercise, flick through the book once again and refresh your memory. Take your time. I don't mind if you spend a few seconds, **1** minute, **1,440** minutes, **2,280** minutes, **43,200** minutes, or **525,600** minutes. Go wild and design a new Table of Contents for me in the blank area below.

What are above numbers in bold? Are these just randomly picked numbers?

TABLE OF CONTENTS

How did you go with your second try on the design of the 'Table of Contents'? Do you like it, more or less, or do you like both?

Anyway, you know what to do – be creative! Make a deal on fonts, colours, drawings, or even remove the Table of Contents. Who said a book must have one and why it has to be called 'Table of Contents'? Or invent a word representing 'Table of Contents', or do whatsoever, just experience things!

And, we are not done yet.

Our activity continues: now imagine this is your book, how would you design the book structure, what title would you use, what contents would you put down? Will that be more interesting, entertaining, educational than mine? Or will that be a fiction, novel, fantasy, or a new genre that nobody knows yet?

Why not start writing your own book, making your own things: YouTube video, cookies, furniture, home decorations and so on. Complete your 'so on' list on the wavy lines here:

～～～～～～～～～～～～～～～～～～～～～～～

～～～～～～～～～～～～～～～～～～～～～～～

～～～～～～～～～～～～～～～～～～～～～～～

Start and continue to live your own creative and artistic life! All you need to do is take bloody action – run for it!

I'm going to show you the standard of Table of Contents next. Is it international standard? Is it kind of boring or the right way to present?

TABLE OF CONTENTS

APPENDIX	1
END	6
∞ Step Three: Explore **YOUR** magic tools!	12
66 - Gather your magic tools	13
65 - Start with a definition	14
64 - Limitation is/isn't a limitation	15
63 - Make math your favourite subject	16
62 - Decode 'From' and 'To'	18
61 - Google is a great assistant, indeed.	19
60 - Look for a pattern	21
59 - Ask questions like [ ]	22
58 - 5Ws and 2Hs	24
57 - What if?	26
56 - Draw out your mind map	27
55 - Tell me stories, please!	30
54 - Bring it on – interesting principles, laws, theories…	32
53 - Say hello to charts and graphs	33
52 - Shapes and colors are your choice	34
51 - Art in different forms	36
50 - Make it sharp and sweet	37
49 - Magic tools – A LOT - INFINITE, basically!	38
∞ Step Two: Upgrade **YOUR** thinking!	40
48 - Creativity is everyone's birthright – no kidding.	41
47 - You are a creative genius!	43
46 - What can you do with your creativity?	44
45 - Create creativity in your day job	45
44 - You are a fabulous creative artist	46
43 - Anything you do is ART	47

TABLE OF CONTENTS

42 - Upgrade your mindset, as a fabulous creative artist	48
41 - Age isn't just a number	49
40 - Present lousy excuses = Future massive regrets	50
39 - Words have their power	51
38 - Is what you see what you see?	52
37 - 720-degree thinking strategy	53
36 - There's never a setback	54
35 - Break your brain's biases	56
34 - You're right, but never assume you're right	57
33 - Your money can be your best friend	58
32 - Appreciate the beauty of imperfection	59
31 - There's always more than one way to 'skin' a 'sheep'	60
30 - Replace self-discipline with self-doing	61
29 - Practise your thinking once again	62
28 - Ways to upgrade your thinking – A LOT – INFINITE, in fact!	65
∞ Step One: Start **YOUR** running, right now!	66
27 - Run for it, RIGHT NOW	67
26 - Sparks creativity in your daily routine	68
25 - Take super-super-super-quick notes	69
24 - Choose an activity, any except…	70
23 - Digital addiction is a new norm?	71
22 - Seriously, you can stop your digital addiction!	72
21 - Put your not-so-good habitsssss into sleep	74
20 - Discover your creativity projectsssss	76
19 - Stack your boxes	77
18 - Have a creative heart of gold	78
17 - Try things	79
16 - Read AMAP	81
15 - Visit art, exhibitions and museums	83

14 - Shout out your bloody hard work	85
13 - Set up a 30-day challenge	86
12 - Play, rest and sleep	87
11 - Celebrate early mornings, or dark nights	88
10 - Do it consistently until...	89
9 - Suck and stuck?	90
8 - Have the patience of a saint	92
7 - Deliver on your commitment	93
6 - Ways to do – A LOT – INFINITE!	95
∞ Step Zero: From Zero to Aero	96
5 - About Zero – a page from my first book	97
4 - About Aero – the same page from my first book	99
3 - About this book	101
2 - About the book title	103
1 - About the ∞	104
0 - About your creativity	105
INTRODUCTION	106
TABLE OF CONTENTS	116
ACKNOWLEDGEMENTS	122
ABOUT THE AUTHOR(S)	123

ACKNOWLEDGEMENTS

To mum and dad, to whoever has or will come across to my life, to Busybird Publishing, Kev Howlett and Les Zigomanis, to whoever cracks open this book, to you, the legend, the fabulous creative artist, or whatever the nickname you prefer.

Put your cute nickname down here – the more, the merrier:

_____

_____

_____

ABOUT THE AUTHOR(S)

After spending nearly 2,000 days of her spare time writing, editing and self-publishing her first book – *The English Builder!: Ace Your English in 365 Days*, Jessie Gao has become addictive to the artist world full of creativity, which she has been practising for years.

This is her second book *Infinite (∞) Ways to Stay Creative!*

Accounting is her profession, and she loves writing, painting, cooking, photographing, doing all-sorts of sports and trying things. CreativeArt_365 and An Excel Pro is her YouTube channel that she created for fun.

Let's move to one of the most exciting parts of this book, put down your name and your bio down in the blank area below (word limit: 200 characters).

Why did we call this 'About the author(s)' page? You're a part of our creation journey throughout and playing a co-author role – it's teamwork! You deserve a big shout out! Only 2% of the world's population will publish a book, so we're all on top of the world now! Wow!

But I can't pay you any royalties, sorry!

www.ingramcontent.com/pod-product-compliance
Lightning Source LLC
Chambersburg PA
CBHW060457080526
44584CB00015B/1463